D0209316

VINDALOO
—AND OTHER—
HOT CURRIES

CURRY CLUB

VINDALOO
—AND OTHER—
HOT CURRIES

PAT CHAPMAN

PIATKUS

First published in 1993 by
Judy Piatkus (Publishers) Limited
5 Windmill Street, London W1P 1HF

The moral right of the author has been asserted

*A catalogue record for this book
is available from the British Library*

ISBN 0-7499-1284-7

Designed by Sue Ryall
Photography by James Murphy

Typeset by Computerset, Harmondsworth, Heathrow
Printed and bound in Great Britain by
Mackays of Chatham PLC

Contents

Foreword

THE CURRY CLUB

Since it was founded in January 1982, The Curry Club has built up a membership of several thousands. Members receive a bright and colourful magazine four times a year, which has regular features on curry and the curry lands. It includes news items, recipes, reports on restaurants, picture features and contributions from members and professionals alike. We have produced a wide selection of publications, including the books on page ii.

Obtaining the ingredients required for Indian cooking can be difficult, but The Curry Club makes it easy, with a comprehensive range of Curry Club products, including spice mixes, chutneys, pickles, papadoms, sauces and curry pastes. These are available from major food stores and specialist delicatessens up and down the country. If they are not stocked near you, there is the Club's well-established and efficient mail-order service. Hundreds of items are stocked, including spices, pastes, gift items, publications and specialist kitchen and tableware.

The Club also holds residential weekend cookery courses and gourmet nights at selected restaurants. Top of the list is our regular gourmet trip to India and other spicy countries. We take a small group of curry enthusiasts to the chosen country and tour the incredible sights, in between sampling the delicious foods of each region.

If you would like more information about **The Curry Club, write (enclosing a SAE) to: The Curry Club, PO Box 7, Haslemere, Surrey GU27 1EP.**

Introduction

The word 'vindaloo', pronounced *vin-deloo* with the emphasis on the first and third syllable, does not appear in my *Concise Oxford Dictionary*. This is hardly surprising as my edition was the second edition which was published in 1929, and even though it was purchased by my mother in Bombay when she used to live there, vindaloo was not then a word in common English usage.

You'd imagine it is a different story today, so I thought I'd better check with the word and language service of the *Oxford Dictionary*. The editor there was quite surprised to find that vindaloo does not appear in the latest (8th, 1990) edition of the *Concise Oxford Dictionary* either. Admitting to an adoration of vindaloo herself, she was considerably relieved to find it in the 20-volume *Oxford English Dictionary*, cost £1650, which says that vindaloo, noun, is 'an Indian curry dish of meat, fish or poultry in a sauce of garlic, wine or vinegar etc,' and that the word is probably of Portuguese origin. *Chambers English Dictionary* tells us that vindaloo is 'a type of very hot Indian curry', while their concise dictionary, like Oxford's, does not define the word. This is a pity because the word is gaining colloquial strength in popular language as a noun, adjective or verb meaning something great, powerful or remarkable. In a recent sports broadcast, I heard the commentator referring to a difficult rugby conversion as a 'vindaloo kick' and aficionados of hot food grade themselves as 'vindaloo men or women.' An estate agent I met a few years ago told me that a prospective house buyer had just been 'vindalooed' – gazumped – by a rival bidder.

At around the same time, news filtered through that the Queen was having problems with pests at Windsor. Rabbits and pigeons were destroying crops on the Windsor Farm. So royal farm manager Bill Gibson came up with a solution. He sprayed curry powder on to the fields to deter the pigeons, and spread lion dung (free from nearby Windsor Safari Park) around seedling crops to fool the rabbits into believing a predator was around. 'It really seems to work,' says Gibson. 'I use a hot curry powder like vindaloo to get up the pigeons' beaks. They don't come back.' In a masterpiece of understatement, a member of the royal retinue described the combination of smells as 'rather powerful'.

But arguably the most intriguing use of the word came from the marketing department at the Ford Motor Company, in a recent poster campaign promoting their best-selling Escort car. The larger-than-life billboards carried pictures of their two top-of-the-range Escorts, the sporty XR3i and the even more powerful RS Cosworth. Only one word of copy described each car: 'Madras' for the XR3i and 'Vindaloo' for the RS. Witty, ingenious, brilliant, hot stuff indeed.

The dictionaries may well adopt a slightly timid approach to the inclusion of words which have long since passed into every-day ordinary speech, but to the people Vindaloo not only exists, it has street credibility, and significant meaning, whether they actually eat it or not.

Curiously enough vindaloo is not the hottest curry on the Indian restaurant menu – that honour goes to the phal curry. Even more curious both vindaloo and phal, and their less hot relative the Madras curry are inventions of Punjabi restaurateurs in Britain. In the early days, when establishing the formula curry house menu, they found there was a demand from their non-Asian diners for curries hotter then they, the restaurateurs themselves, were willing or able to eat. These mild men from the north of the sub-continent looked southwards for inspiration and came up with 'product' names from places they knew served hot food, but which they themselves had probably never visited. Madras, largest city in southern India supplied one suitable name (add 1 teaspoon chilli powder to a basic medium curry recipe). Vindaloo originated in Goa on India's South west coast, (add two teaspoons chilli). Phal seems simply to mean 'hot' in the Sylhet district of Bangladesh, where most UK curry restaurateurs come from (add 3 or more teaspoons).

Despite the Oxford Dictionary hedging its bets as to the probable origin of the word, there can be no doubt whatever about its Portuguese ancestry, according to Kenneth Grisham, an American Oxford post-graduate etymologist, specialising in Hindi and Urdu food words. Now resident in Dallas, Kenneth took me to task a few years ago for mis-defining vindaloo. I thought that **'aloo'** referred to potato. Indeed nearly all the 7,500 curry houses up and down the UK and those in the USA, Australia and elsewhere also believe this to be the case. They all serve huge chunks of potato in their vindaloo curries, 'aloo' meaning potato in many Indian languages. Not so, says Kenneth. 'This word has nothing to do with potatoes; it comes from Portuguese **vinha d'alhos** and refers to a dish made with vinegar and garlic (**alho**). The dish is well known in Portugal.' And of course, I should have known this, because the original dish came from Goa, which became a Portuguese colony in 1496, long before the British arrived in India. The Goan dish is pronounced *vin-dar-loo*, with the emphasis on the second syllable. Because the population was, like-it-or-not, converted to Christianity by the Portuguese, the Moslem taboo of pork was dispelled and pigs, indispensable to the Portuguese, were introduced. Authentic vindaloo always and only uses pork, which is marinated in vinegar (with massive quantities of garlic, chillies and other spices) in barrels, sometimes for days, even months, before being simmered to cook. Potatoes never appear in the authentic vindaloo, for which a recipe appears on page 24.

If vindaloo has many strengths as a word, it also, sadly has weaknesses. It is the subject of innumerable lavatorial weak jokes, which in no way helps its image. And it has become linked with the type of diner readers of this page totally abhor: the lager lout. A seemingly indispensable part of Saturday-night-out for these specimens is to continue to swill alcohol, after throwing-out time at the pub, by going to the local curry house, for a further 8 pints of vindaloo and even more lagers, coupled with as much racial taunting as they can achieve. Restaurants wishing not to associate themselves with this image shut their doors well before the pubs close, but sadly economic necessity leave many others no alternative but to take these creatures' money. One presumes the staff can cope, although I often speculate that the UK vindaloo and its close relatives were created out of spite as a punishment for such customers.

Be that as it may, curry in general and vindaloo in particular still suffers a down-market image due almost entirely to the lager lout. Ironically, the restaurateurs' punishment back-fired (excuse the weak joke) because, even though the restaurateurs themselves may not eat hot food, others do, as we shall see. The phenomenon of addiction to hot food is worldwide, and eating hot curries is regarded as not in the least bit masochistic by those who enjoy them, even, presumably the lager louts.

Let us look more closely at what heat is, why we enjoy its effects, whether it is indeed addictive and whether it is harmful.

ABOUT 'HOT' FOOD

In the English language heat, unfortunately has two totally unrelated meanings – temperature and piquancy. This gives the author of cookery books problems, and I hope that no ambiguities exist in my text. In this chapter heat and hot refer exclusively to piquancy.

Heat is a measurable amount of piquancy in certain ingredients. The ones used in this book are, in ascending order (hottest last), ginger, onion, garlic, pepper, mustard and chilli, although some varieties of onion can be mild and others quite hot.

The chemical which causes heat in chillies is called capsicin. Dave Dewitt from Albuquerque, editor of *Chile Pepper Magazine* and author of *The Whole Chile Pepper Book* defines capsicin as 'an incredibly powerful and stable alkaloid seemingly unaffected by cold or heat, which retains its original potency over time, cooking, or freezing. Because it has no flavour, colour, or odour, the precise amount of capsicin present in chillies can only be measured by a specialized laboratory procedure.' Wilbur Scoville in 1912 developed this process which places chillies in a scale of 0 to 10 (see below).

Chillies

Chillies originated in Central and Latin America (where they were and are called chiles) and were 'discovered' by the Spanish and Portuguese voyagers of the fifteenth century.

Prior to that the rest of the world heated up its food with pepper. It is hard to believe that India, the Orient and North Africa did not have the chilli until then. But within decades of their American 'discovery' they were indispensable to the diet of most of the tropical world.

There are at least 150 varieties of chilli worldwide, although we generally encounter just a few of them.

Cayenne is the chilli most commonly encountered in curry cooking. The variety found in UK shops is long and thin, about $2^1/_2$ inches to 4 inches (6.25-10 cm) by $^1/_2$ inch (1.25 cm), is green or red and rates 8 on the Scoville scale. Tiny cayenne chillies about 1 inch (2.5 cm) long are used in Thai cooking and rate 8-9 on the same scale.

Long green chillies (about 6-8 inches / 15-20 cm) are the **Anaheim** or **New Mexico** variety, with a heat rating of 2-4.

Bird, birdseye, tepin or **Ugandan** chillies are tiny, available red dried and occasionally fresh, and rate 8-9.

The small stubby (2¹/₂ inch / 6.25 cm) green or red chillies are **Jalapēno**, rating 5.

Hottest of all are **Haberno** chillies. Rating 10, they are 1-2¹/₂ inches (2.5-6.25 cm) long × 1-2 inches (2.5-5 cm) wide. Of irregular heart shape, also called the **Scotch Bonnet, Jamaican** and **Bahama Mama**, they are available fresh in the UK.

Chilli Powder

It is perhaps less well known, that as with chillies, chilli powder can vary dramatically in heat rating. Some of the recipes in this book specify a particular type of powder such as 'extra hot chilli powder' which is made from bird chillies. Cayenne should be quite hot and ground from dried cayenne chillies. Barts Spices cayenne pepper uses only peppers but it must measure 8 on the Scoville heat scale. However, some manufacturers add cummin powder and other spices to create a blend under the name cayenne. The best advice is to shop around until you find products which you like, then stick with them.

Addiction

Over half the world's population enjoy hot spicy food. It is no coincidence that chillies are so important to so many people. If you have read this chapter so far, you will be among them, and you'll know that only people who do not eat hot food claim that heat masks all other flavours. Heat addicts know that this could not be further from the truth. Furthermore, the detractors state that eating hot food is detrimental to health, even carcinogenic. Those of us who enjoy hot curries know that we need a regular fix from time to time, the more serious the addiction the more often the fix. But are we curryholics endangering ourselves and why are we addicted?

Recent serious studies have been carried out by Australian, American and British scientists. It seems that they have become concerned about the effects eating spices have in terms of addiction. They confirm what the curryholic already knows well – curry is addictive! In a serious study at the Senory Research Centre in Sydney a group of 35 scientists, led by a Dr Prescott, voluntarily underwent a two year programme of regular curry eating, during which time they were measured for the stimulation that intense flavourings such as capsicin have on the trigeminal nerve, when combined with sucrose and sodium chloride. Or in lay terms what chilli, sugar and salt do to the taste buds. As everyone knows eating chilli can be painful, especially to those not used to it. Capsicin is the heat-giving agent, or pain element in chilli and spices.

The findings were that capsicin, unlike sugar and salt, gives an enormous boost of intensity to taste. At the same time it causes the release of endorphins, the body's natural pain killers. Endorphins can give a person a feeling of pleasure and well-being. In brief, say the scientists, you get a 'buzz' from eating capsicin. Furthermore, they point out, because the body becomes used to the exposure, it increases the level of endorphins it releases. And so, say the scientists, eating spicy foods becomes addictive. They end their report with a reassuring bit of *good* news, 'it is unlikely that eating too many spicy foods will damage the trigeminal nerve' and *bad* news, 'the first bite of a mild curry leads to the vindaloo!'

Another serious work involving capsicin and spices led to Mexican Benigno Villalon obtaining his Ph. D (as a plant pathologist) on the subject. Known to his colleagues at the Texas A and M University as 'Dr Pepper', Villalon has found that eating chilli and spicy foods does not cause stomach ulcers, nor any other disease or infection. At the University of California Los Angeles, professor of medicine Irwin Zimet routinely prescribes chilli peppers and other pungent food, ie: curry, to his patients suffering from colds, coughs and other respiratory ailments. 'Chilli loosens up the mucus in the throat and lungs,' he says 'and a lot of expensive drugs don't have any more proven abilities than chillies do.'

Another group of American scientists, at the behest of McCormick and Co., the world's largest spice company, have tested how heat affects the mouth. Chilli, they say, burns the tongue, ginger burns the throat. Red pepper lessens the taste of sour and bitter and black pepper inhibits all tastes.

In the midst of all this euphoria the British have come out with a guarded bit of pessimism. The West Midlands Health Authority recently announced that in their view pregnant women ought not to eat curry. It may, they say, impede the development of the foetus. It makes you wonder how 24 million babies are born each year in curry-eating India.

Indeed all these statistics make the curryholic smile. Those of us who enjoy the odd chilli and the odd curry know we're hooked. Still, I suppose we should rejoice in the fact that these things are being taken seriously. One just wonders how many curries it took all those earnest researchers to come to their conclusions. Maybe they are all confirmed curryholics themselves.

Pepper

Pepper, *piper nigrum*, has for thousands of years been India's King of Spices – her major spice and revenue earner and it still remains an important heat additive in her cuisine. Peppercorns are the fruit or berries of the pepper vine which grows only in monsoon forests. The heart-shaped leaves (*paan*) are used as a digestive. The vine flowers triennially and it produces berries, called spikes, in long clusters, first green then changing colour through from yellow to orange-red and eventually to crimson when ripe. Depending on the colour of the spikes when cropped, you will get green, black, white or pink peppercorns, for they are all one and the same thing. Green peppercorns are very immature, and are either bottled in vinegar or brine immediately in order to retain their colour, or are air-dried or, more recently, freeze-dried. To obtain black peppercorns, the spikes are picked when they start changing colour to yellow. They are dried in the sun and within a day or so become black and shrivelled. To harvest white pepper, the spikes are left on the vines until they turn red. The outer red skin is removed by soaking it off, revealing an inner white berry which is then dried. Pink (red) pepper is obtained in the same way from a specific variety of vine, and it is immediately air-dried to prevent it turning white.

WHAT TO SERVE WITH HOT CURRIES

Most of the recipes in this book are for hot meat, poultry, fish and vegetable main course dishes. It comes as no surprise to those who are used to hot dishes, that they accompany them with more (even hotter) hot things. For example you can serve the mustard rice dish on page 58 and/or the chilli chapatti on page 59, with hot chutneys on pages 61-3. In my other curry books listed on page ii you will find a greater selection of accompaniments, most of them not hot.

Antidotes to Heat

Research shows that milk is more effective than water in cooling a mouth on fire because your food is too hot. Yoghurt is even better and acts faster than milk or water to put out the fire. See pages 62-3 for some yoghurt raitas to serve with your curries.

Garnishes

These can be as simple or extravagant as you like. The options are endless but here are a few ideas: a simple sprinkling of chilli powder or chopped fresh herbs, lemon or lime wedges, thinly sliced chillies, toasted nuts or even a salad garnish. Chilli tassels (page 60) are simple to make and very effective. Some recipes specify a particular garnish but for the most part the choice is yours.

Drink

This is a personal choice. I like red wine with hot curries although experts disagree about this. It should not be fine wine – a cheap and cheerful plonk will do the meal great justice in my view. Rosé, white wine, sparkling wine and real ale are also appropriate. Most lagers are too gassy, although Cobra Lager brewed in Bangalore is designed to go with curry. I should warn you however that chilli, and alcohol, both can cause dehydration, so drink plenty of water before going to sleep. Non-alcoholic drinks are always acceptable.

USING THESE RECIPES

If at any time during the cooking a curry seems too dry, add a little water and maybe some oil too to maintain the gravy. If it seems too wet just carry on stir-frying until the water reduces. Many recipes require frequent adjustment of the hob's temperature. In general the initial spice and garlic stir-fry should be over high heat, but long stir-fries (of onions or main ingredients) should be over a lower heat.

Opposite (top to bottom): Cold Chilli Chana (**page 10**), Hot 'n' Spicy Salad (**page 15**), Red Chilli Tomato Soup (**page 7**), and Mirchi Masala Omelette (**page 8**)

Opposite page 1 (top to bottom): Meat Vindaloo (**page 18**), Sweet Red Chilli Chutney (**page 62**), and Goan Pork Vindaloo (**pages 24-5**) garnished with lightly toasted flakes of coconut and shredded red chilli

CHAPTER · 1

Ingredients and Basic Recipes

INGREDIENTS

Most of the fresh and dried ingredients in this book are widely available from supermarkets and delicatessens. If you have problems obtaining any of the specialist ingredients such as ghee, coconut milk, tamarind and of course all the spices listed below, they are available, along with much much more, by mail order – see page vi.

SPICES

It is the combination of spices which makes the cooking of the sub-continent of India so special. Vindaloo and hot curry cooking is no exception. The spices you will need to make these recipes are not too many, neither will they cost you too much. Yet they are crucial to all which follows, so they should be cared for as if they were gold. There are some rules.

Firstly Buy in small quantities. Once their packets are opened, the spices deteriorate and eventually lose all their flavour (or essential oils). Use them within 6-12 months of opening for ground spices and 12-18 months for whole spices. Beyond those dates, bin them and buy fresh.

Secondly Store in an airtight lidded container, in a dry place. Temperature is not important, but it is better cooler rather than hotter.

Thirdly Do not be tempted to display your spices in alluring glass jars. Ultraviolet and especially direct sunlight fades the colours and, more important, the tastes. Spices are best kept in a dark place — a cupboard or pantry.

THE SPICES YOU NEED

The following list will enable you to make all the dishes in this book; an asterisk indicates that the particular spice is used in only one or two recipes. All of these spices are available by mail order. See page vi for details.

Whole Spices

anise, star (saunf star) *
bay leaves (tej patia)
cardamom black/brown (elaichi burra)
cardamom white/green (elaichi chota)
cassia bark (dalchini)
chillies whole, red, dried (lal mirch)
cloves (lavang)
coriander seeds (dhania)
cummin seeds, white (jeera)
fennel seeds (soonf)
fenugreek leaves, dried (tej methi)
fenugreek seeds (methi) *
lovage seeds (ajwain or ajowan) *
mace blades (javitri) *
mustard seeds, black (kala rai)
onion seeds, wild (nigella or kalongi)
peppercorns, black (mirch)
pomegranate (ardrana) *
poppy seeds, white (cuscus)
sesame seeds, white (til)

Ground Spices

Some spices are best bought as factory ground spices:
asafoetida (hing)

chilli powder (lal mirch)
coriander (dhania)
cummin (jeera)
mango powder (am chur) *
mustard powder (rai)
paprika
pepper, black (mirch)
turmeric (huldi)

ROASTING SPICES

Some recipes in this book call for roasted spices. Roasting spices is easy and it's fun and the results you get are stupendous. The analogy is coffee. The 'roasting' process releases those delicious aromatic fragrances, the essential oils, into the air.

The simplest way to 'roast' spices is to put them in a pre-heated dry frying pan or wok which you put on a medium heat on the stove. Dry stir-fry (no oil or water, remember) for 30-60 seconds to release the aromas. Do not let the spices burn, and if they do then bin them – it's cheap enough and quick enough to start again. Cool the spices. You can store them, but it is better to roast them and use them immediately as required.

GRINDING SPICES

Roast them first and cool them. Then grind in a mortar and pestle if you enjoy hard work, or in a coffee grinder or spice mill.

GARAM MASALA

— ◆ —

This is the best example of roasting and grinding your own spices. Try it, at least once, please. Then compare it with any brand of factory-made garam masala. I guarantee you'll do-it-yourself from then on.

Garam means hot; masala, mixture of spices. The heat comes from the pepper. There are as many mixtures as there are cooks, but all should use aromatic spices. This version is a little hotter than most, having been formulated for those who like heat. Next time you may wish to add other spices or make other changes.

Garam masala is best used towards the end of the cooking. Add it too early, and you lose its aromatic qualities. It can also be sprinkled over a finished dish as a garnish. I've used metric weights only. Tablespoons (heaped) are acceptable but less accurate.

Makes 260 g (about 17 heaped tablespoons when ground)

60 g (9 heaped tablespoons) coriander seeds

40 g (4 heaped tablespoons) cummin seeds

40 g (4 heaped tablespoons) black peppercorns

30 g (4 heaped tablespoons) dried red chillies

30 g (several pieces) cassia bark

30 g (3 heaped tablespoons) brown cardamom

30 g (6 heaped tablespoons) clove

Lightly roast everything under a low-medium grill or in a low oven. Do not let the spices burn. They should give off a light steam. When they give off an aroma, remove from the heat, cool and grind in batches.

After grinding, mix thoroughly and store in an airtight jar. Garam masala will last almost indefinitely, but it is always better to make small batches every few months to get the best flavours.

HOT CURRY PASTE

—— ◆ ——

Many of the recipes in this book call for hot curry paste.
You can use any bottled hot curry paste. The Curry Club
sells Vindaloo Curry Paste in 190 g jars, for example,
formulated to my own recipe. For those who prefer to
make their own, here is a really hot recipe. I've used
precise measures in metric only and approximate measures in heaped spoonfuls.

Makes: about 16 oz (450 g) paste

60 g (4 tablespoons)
  coriander

55 g (4 tablespoons) chilli
  powder

20 g (4 teaspoons) cummin

20 g (4 teaspoons) garam
  masala

15 g (3 teaspoons) turmeric

8 g (1¹/₂ teaspoons)
  fenugreek seeds, ground

8 g (1¹/₂ teaspoons) fennel
  seeds, ground

7 g (1¹/₄ teaspoons) ginger
  powder

7 g (1¹/₄ teaspoons) yellow
  mustard

8 fl oz (250 ml) water

4¹/₂ fl oz (125 ml) distilled
  clear vinegar

5 fl oz (150 ml) corn oil

Mix the ground spices together. Add the vinegar and
water and mix into a paste. Leave it for 15 minutes.

In a large pan, heat the oil. Add the paste (careful of the
spluttering), lower the heat and stir-fry for 5-10 minutes.
As the liquid is reduced, the paste will begin to make a
regular bubbling noise (hard to describe, but it goes chup-
chup-chup-chup) if you don't stir, and it will splatter.
This is your audible cue that it is ready. You can tell if the
spices are cooked by taking the pan off the stove. Leave to
stand for 3-4 minutes. If the oil 'floats' to the top, the
spices are cooked. If not, add a little more oil and repeat.

Bottle the paste in sterilised jars. Then heat up a little
more oil and 'cap' off the paste by pouring in enough oil
to cover. Seal the jars and store. Properly cooked, it will
last indefinitely.

CHAPTER 2

The Hot Start

Indians are great snack eaters, which is not surprising because the range of tasty morsels they have to choose from is stupendous. This tiny selection can be served as snacks in their own right or as starters. What they all have in common is a high level of 'heat'.

GREEN PEPPER RASAM SOUP

A South Indian consommé-style, fiery soup.

Serves: 4

2 tablespoons sesame oil
2 garlic cloves, thinly sliced
2 oz (50 g) Spanish onion, thinly sliced
1¹/₃ pints (800 ml) water
2 tablespoons vinegar (any type)
1 tablespoon red lentils
2 oz (50 g) spinach, thinly sliced
6 green chillies, thinly sliced
2 tablespoons chopped fresh coriander leaves

sugar
salt
chilli powder

SPICES

1 teaspoon sesame seeds
1 teaspoon mustard seeds
¹/₂ teaspoon turmeric
2 bay leaves
6 curry leaves (optional)
2 teaspoons bottled green peppercorns

Heat the oil in a 3$^{1}/_{3}$ pint (1.9l) saucepan and fry the **spices** for 20 seconds. Add the garlic, then after 20 seconds add the onion. Stir-fry for 5 minutes. Add the measured water, the vinegar, lentils, spinach, chillies and most of the coriander. Simmer for 25-30 minutes. Sugar and salt to taste. Serve sprinkled with chilli powder and the remaining fresh coriander leaves.

RED CHILLI TOMATO SOUP

— ◆ —

Indian hot spices pep up this old favourite.

Serves: 4

2 tablespoons light vegetable oil

2 garlic cloves, finely chopped

2 oz (50 g) Spanish onion, finely chopped

14 oz (400 g) can tomato soup

14 fl oz (400 ml) tomato juice

4 fl oz (100 ml) red wine

2 tablespoons tomato ketchup

2 teaspoons Worcester sauce

1 tablespoon vinegar (any type)

$^{1}/_{2}$-2 tablespoons minced red chilli (page 60)

sugar and salt to taste

2 or 3 fresh red chillies, finely chopped (optional)

12-16 fresh coriander leaves

SPICES

1 teaspoon paprika

$^{1}/_{2}$ teaspoon cummin

$^{1}/_{2}$ teaspoon coriander

$^{1}/_{2}$ teaspoon mustard seeds

Heat the oil in a 3$^{1}/_{3}$ pint (1.9l) saucepan and fry the **spices** for 20 seconds. Add the garlic, then after 20 seconds add the onion. Stir-fry for 5 minutes. Add the tomato soup, tomato juice, red wine, ketchup, Worcester sauce, vinegar and minced red chilli. Mix well and simmer for 10 minutes. Sugar and salt to taste and garnish with the optional red chillies and coriander leaves.

MIRCHI MASALA OMELETTE

— ◆ —

Chopped green chillies, onion and fresh coriander make this omelette memorable. Indians have it for breakfast, and so do I.

Serves: 1

1 tablespoon butter
1 garlic clove, thinly sliced
1 oz (25 g) onion, thinly
    sliced
$^1/_4$ teaspoon turmeric
2-4 green chillies, chopped
2 teaspoons chopped fresh
    coriander leaves

$^1/_2$ tomato, chopped
2 large eggs
black pepper, freshly ground
salt to taste
shredded red chilli to garnish
a sprig of fresh coriander or
    flat leaf parsley to garnish

Heat the butter in a flat frying pan. Stir-fry the garlic, onion, turmeric, chillies, coriander and tomato for about 2 minutes. Meanwhile, briskly beat the eggs, then pour them into the pan, swirling it around so that the egg rolls right round it. Cook for a couple of minutes, until the omelette is firm, then serve sprinkled with pepper and salt to taste and lashings of red chilli to garnish. Top with a sprig of coriander or parsley.

COLD HOT CHILLI POTATO

— ◆ —

Served cold, spiced hot, the humble potato comes alive.

Serves: 4 as a starter

1 lb (450 g) potatoes, boiled
    and cooled
1 tablespoon bottled
    tandoori paste
1 tablespoon minced red
    chilli (page 60)
4 oz (110 g) onion, finely
    chopped
1 teaspoon cummin seeds,
    roasted
1 tablespoon chilli pickle,
    chopped (page 61)

1 tablespoon chopped fresh
    coriander leaves
$1/2$ teaspoon mango powder
salt to taste

GARNISH

1 teaspoon garam masala
    (page 4)
squeeze of fresh lemon juice
shredded fresh green chilli

Chop the cold boiled potatoes into $1/2$ inch (1.25 cm) cubes and put them into a large bowl. Add the other ingredients, mix and leave to marinate in the fridge for an hour. Garnish and serve.

COLD CHILLI CHANA

— ◆ —

Another starter/snack served cold. The versatile chickpea is the star, chilli sauce the support act.

Serves: 4 as a starter

14 oz (400 g) can chickpeas
14 oz (400 g) can plum tomatoes
1 tablespoon pistachio oil
1 tablespoon hot curry paste (page 5)
1 garlic clove, finely chopped
4 oz (110 g) onion, finely chopped
2 tablespoons mango chutney, finely chopped
6-8 fresh green chillies, chopped
1 tablespoon garam masala (page 4)
2 tablespoons tomato ketchup
salt to taste

GARNISH
desiccated coconut
a red chilli if available

Drain the chickpeas. (Use the liquid for stock for another dish.) Do the same with the tomatoes, then chop them up. Put the chickpeas and tomatoes in a bowl and mix in the remaining ingredients. Salt to taste and leave for an hour or two in the fridge to marinate. Garnish and serve.

CHILLI AND PEPPER SHEEK KEBAB

— ◆ —

Lean meat ground with garlic, ginger, spices and chilli and reinforced with green pepper, shaped into sausages and cooked. Mouthwatering tingly tastes.

Serves: 4

$1^{1}/_{2}$ *lb (675 g) best lean steak*
4 garlic cloves, chopped
1 inch (2.5 cm) cube fresh ginger, chopped
6-8 fresh green chillies, chopped
2 tablespoons chopped fresh coriander leaves

2 tablespoons bottled green peppercorns
1 tablespoon dried onion flakes
1 tablespoon garam masala (page 4)
1 teaspoon salt
2 tablespoons bottled tandoori paste

Cut the meat into 1 inch (2.5 cm) cubes, discarding all unwanted matter. Run it through the mincer two or three times, or chop it in the food processor, until it is smooth textured. Mix in the other ingredients and run it through the machine once more ensuring it is well mixed.

Divide the mixture into four and shape into sausages. Either place each sausage on a skewer and grill or bar-becue them, or cook them in an oven preheated to 375°F/190°C/Gas 5 for 15 minutes. Serve on a bed of Hot 'n' Spicy Salad (page 15) with Coconut Raita (page 63) and lemon wedges.

GREEN CHILLI CHICKEN KEBABS

—— ◆ ——

Chicken breast chunks marinated in a pureé of green herbs and fresh chilli for 48 hours. Then they are skewered and cooked. Great for the barbecue!

Serves: 4

$1^1/2$ lb (675 g) fresh not frozen filleted chicken breast, cut into 20-24 cubes of $1^1/2$ inch (2.5 cm) (see note below)
lemon wedges

MARINADE
16 oz (450 g) yoghurt
4 cloves garlic
1 inch (2.5 cm) cube fresh ginger
1 bunch fresh coriander leaves, chopped
8 oz (225 g) mint leaves

1 green pepper, pith and seeds discarded
4 tablespoons chilli pickle (page 61)
4-6 fresh green chillies
8 oz (225 g) spring onion leaves
2 tablespoons dried onion flakes
1 tablespoon garam masala (page 4)
2 teaspoons salt
milk as required

Put the marinade ingredients into the blender, using milk if necessary to mulch down into a pale green pourable paste. Transfer this to a large non-metallic bowl, then mix in the chicken. Cover and leave in the fridge to marinate for 48 hours

Pre-heat the grill to medium. Slip the marinated chicken on to four skewers, allowing five or six pieces each. Place the skewers on an oven rack above the grill tray, and place this in the midway position under the heat. Alternatively barbecue them. Cook for 5 minutes, turn and repeat. Cut one piece to ensure it is fully cooked (white throughout). If not, cook for a while longer. Serve on a bed of Hot 'n' Spicy Salad (page 15) with Chilli Chapatti (page 59), lemon wedges and chutney.

CHILLI ONION PAKORAS

A tasty spicy fritter – the onion *bhajee* or *bhajia* really, under another name, but supplemented with chopped chilli to the level of your endurance.

Makes: 8 pakoras

4 oz (110 g) gram flour (besan)
2 fl oz (50 ml) lemon juice
oil for deep frying
8 oz (225 g) onion, finely chopped
2-3 tablespoons minced green chilli (page 60)
1 teaspoon bottled vinegared mint
1 tablespoon hot curry paste (page 5)

1 tablespoon garam masala (page 4)
1 tablespoon chopped fresh coriander leaves
1 teaspoon salt
1 teaspoon cummin seeds, roasted
1/2 teaspoon lovage seeds, roasted
1/3 teaspoon coriander seeds, roasted

Mix the gram flour with the lemon juice and just enough water to make it into a thick paste which will just drop off a spoon. Let it stand for 10 minutes or so to allow the moisture to be fully absorbed by the flour.

Preheat the deep frying oil to 375°C/190°C (chip frying temperature). Add the onion and all the remaining ingredients to the gram flour mixture and stir well. Spoon out 1/8 of the mixture and carefully place it into the hot oil. Repeat with the remaining mixture to make eight pakoras in all, allowing 10-15 seconds between each to enable the oil to retain its temperature. Fry for 10 minutes, turning at least once. Remove from the oil, drain well and serve with salad, lemon wedges and chutneys.

CHINGRI TEMPORADU

— ◆ —

A Sri Lankan delicacy, brought there from Portugal. King prawns marinated in chilli sauce then 'floured' and deep fried. Tingly Chingri indeed!

Serves: 4 as a starter

4 shelled Bengal Tiger prawns, each about 3 oz (75 g), or 12 shelled King prawns, each about 1 oz (25 g)
a sprinkling of chilli powder, to garnish
lemon wedges, to garnish

MARINADE
2 oz (50 g) minced red chilli (page 60)

4 fl oz (100 ml) red wine
1 tablespoon garam masala (page 4)

SPICY FLOUR
4 tablespoons plain white flour
2 tablespoons semolina
2 tablespoons coconut milk powder
2 teaspoons chilli powder

If the prawns are frozen, ensure they are well thawed. Cut away the vein running down the back. Mix the chilli with the wine and garam masala and immerse the prawns in the marinade. Cover and leave in the fridge for a couple of hours.

To cook, pre-heat the deep fryer to 375°F/190°C (chip frying temperature). Mix together the ingredients for the spicy flour. Remove the first prawn, from its marinade, dunk it in the spicy flour mixture, then place it at once into the deep fryer. Repeat with the other prawns. Deep-fry for 6-10 minutes (depending on prawn size), then remove and drain on kitchen paper. Serve garnished with chilli powder and lemon wedges.

HOT 'N' SPICY SALAD

— ◆ —

Pick 'n' mix 'n' chop your choice of salad vegetables. Add your hot 'n' spicy bit (the chillies) and the lemon 'n' pistachio nut oil dressing, 'n' here's a salad which is top of the hots.

Serves: 4 to accompany a starter dish

3 or 4 leaves curly endive
4-6 leaves radicchio
1 bunch watercress
¹/₄ punnet mustard cress
2-4 green chillies
2-4 red chillies
4 inch (10 cm) piece white radish (mooli)
1 tablespoon fresh whole coriander leaves
¹/₂ fennel bulb
6-8 mange touts

2 oz (50 g) red onion, thinly sliced

DRESSING
2 fl oz (50 ml) pistachio oil
2 fl oz (50 ml) fresh lemon juice
2 fl oz (50 ml) white wine
2 fl oz (50 ml) water
1 teaspoon mustard powder
1 teaspoon black pepper
¹/₂ teaspoon cayenne pepper
¹/₂ teaspoon salt

Wash and dry the salad vegetables and chop them as you want them. Put them in a large glass mixing bowl, cover and keep in the fridge for up to 4 hours. Mix together the ingredients for the dressing (it will keep indefinitely so you can make larger amounts if you wish).

Just prior to serving, mix the dressing well and pour it over the salad. Toss the salad and serve at once.

—— ◆ ——

CHAPTER 3

Vindaloo and Other Restaurant Favourites

The standard Indian restaurant menu is generally 'heat' graded. Under 'hot' and 'extra hot' will appear *Madras* and *phal*. *Vindaloo* is generally somewhere in between, with *bindaloo* and *tindaloo* hotter variations, though not at hot as *phal*.

To make these restaurant-style hot curries, you'll need to make a thick soup-like gravy, or sauce, called the 'base'. Here it is in a four-portion serving. This same base is used for all the eight curries in this chapter. Adjustments to times and methods enable the reader to use meat or poultry or seafood or vegetables or combinations.

CURRY BASE GRAVY

—— ◆ ——

Every curry restaurant makes its own base. It is the equivalent of the stock pot in the French or English restaurant kitchen. They are all much of a muchness, but this particular tasty version is a modification of a base worked out by Curry Club member, and sauce super sleuth, Bruce Edwards.

Serves: 4 when added to 1^1/$_2$ lb (675 g) of main ingredient

Makes: 2 pints (1.2 l) sauce

2 garlic cloves
1 inch (2.5 cm) cube fresh
  ginger
1 lb (450 g) Spanish onions
1 medium-sized carrot
1 stick celery
1 tablespoon chopped red
  pepper
4 green chillies
1 tomato
2 inch (5 cm) cube white
  radish (mooli)
2 tablespoons chopped fresh
  coriander leaves

5 tablespoons vegetable oil
1 pint (600 ml) vegetable
  stock or water
$^1/_2$ pint (300 ml) milk

SPICES
1 teaspoon coriander
1 teaspoon turmeric
1 teaspoon cummin
1 teaspoon cayenne pepper
1 teaspoon aromatic curry
  powder
$^1/_3$ teaspoon lovage seeds

Mix the **spices** with 2 tablespoons water. Finely chop all the vegetables. In a 5 pint (2.8 l) saucepan, heat the oil to near smoking, then lower the heat and stir-fry the garlic for 20 seconds. Add the ginger, and 20 seconds later add the spice mixture (be careful of the spluttering). Briskly stir-fry for a minute or so, then add the onions and stir-fry for 10 minutes. Add the stock or water and milk and bring to a gentle simmer. Add the vegetables. Simmer with the lid on for 30 minutes or more – timing here isn't crucial.

Allow to cool down then pass the mixture through the blender to achieve a pourable gravy, sauce or purée. You may need to add a little water here (or earlier) to obtain the correct texture. The curry base is now ready.

Opposite page 16 (top to bottom): Burmese Meat Chilli Fry (**pages 32-3**), Minced Green Chilli (**pages 60-1**), and Thai Lamb Green Curry (**page 27**) garnished with red chillies

Opposite (top to bottom): Thai Turkey Orange Curry (**page 40**), Nepalese River Duck (**page 39**), both garnished with Fresh Chilli Tassels (**page 60**). Alongside are Thai eggplants and tiny Thai pea eggplants

MEAT VINDALOO

—— ◆ ——

This is the archetypal, world-famous, most popular restaurant dish, the title of this book; beloved by some, dreaded and never eaten by most! Pronounced VIN-deLOO, with emphasis on the first and last syllables, it is a hot restaurant invention containing potato (aloo). To find out about the real version, to which this bears no resemblance, see pages ix and 24.

Serves: 4

1¼ lb (560 g) stewing steak or lamb, diced

4 tablespoons ghee or vegetable oil

1 tablespoon tomato purée

2 teaspoons hot curry paste (page 5)

½ teaspoon dry fenugreek leaves

8 red cayenne chillies, cut into long slices

½ green pepper, cut into ½ inch (1.25 cm) cubes

2 pints (1.2 l) curry base gravy (page 16)

8-10 1 inch (2.5 cm) cubes boiled potato

1 tablespoon vinegar (any type)

2 teaspoons garam masala, optional (page 4)

2 tablespoons chopped fresh coriander leaves

salt to taste

SPICES

1½ teaspoons coriander

1 teaspoon cummin

1 teaspoon cayenne pepper

½ teaspoon turmeric

Preheat the oven to 375°F/190°C/Gas 5. Mix the **spices** with 2 tablespoons of water. Heat half the ghee or oil in a pan (karahi, wok or frying pan). Add the spice mixture (it will splutter) and briskly stir-fry for a minute or so, then stir-fry in the tomato purée, curry paste, fenugreek leaves, chillies, green pepper and curry base gravy. When simmering, transfer to a 4½ pint (2.6 l) minimum lidded casserole and put it into the oven.

Now 'seal' the meat by stir-frying it in the pan with the rest of the ghee or oil, for about 10 minutes. Drain off any liquid (keep it for stock or use later) then put the hot meat into the casserole dish. Stir well, put on the lid and replace the dish in the hot oven. After about 20 minutes inspect, stir and add a little heated stock or water if needed.

Continue to cook for another 20 minutes, then inspect again, this time testing for tenderness – it will probably need a little longer. Add the boiled potato cubes, vinegar, garam masala and half the fresh coriander and cook for at least 10 more minutes.

So the total oven time is 50 minutes minimum.

When the meat is as tender as you want it, and just prior to serving, spoon off any excess oil. Salt to taste, garnish with the remaining fresh coriander and serve.

CHICKEN VINDALOO

Use 1¼ lb (560 g) skinless, filleted chicken breast, cut into 1½ inch (4 cm) cubes, instead of meat. The remaining ingredients are the same.

Follow the same method as for meat but cook in the oven for only 20 minutes before adding the potato cubes, etc. So the total oven time is about 30 minutes.

PRAWN, LOBSTER OR SCAMPI VINDALOO

Use 1¼ lb (560 g) whole shelled prawns or king prawns, or lobster meat, scampi etc. (thawed if frozen). The remaining ingredients are the same.

Follow the same method as for meat but cook in the over for only 20 minutes before adding the potato cubes, etc. So the total oven time is about 30 minutes.

TINDALOO/BINDALOO

Restaurant variations on the vindaloo theme. The name of the game is to achieve a curry which is hotter still.

Simply add 1 or 2 or more teaspoons cayenne pepper or extra hot (bird) chilli powder to the spices on page 18. Every other detail is the same.

PHAL/BANGALORE PHAL

— ◆ —

This is the hottest restaurant curry of all.

Serves: 4

1¹/₂ lb (675 g) stewing steak
  or lamb, diced
4 tablespoons ghee or
  vegetable oil
1 tablespoon hot curry paste
  (page 5)
1 tablespoon tomato purée
1 tablespoon tomato ketchup
2 or 3 canned plum tomatoes
1-2 tablespoons minced red
  chilli (page 60)
12 red cayenne chillies, finely
  chopped

2 pints (1.2 l) curry base
  gravy (page 16)
1 tablespoon garam masala
  (page 4)
salt to taste

SPICES

2-3 teaspoons extra hot
  (bird) chilli powder
1 teaspoon coriander
1 teaspoon cummin
¹/₂ teaspoon turmeric

Preheat the oven to 375°F/190°C/Gas 5. Mix the **spices** with 2 tablespoons of water. Heat half the ghee or oil in a pan. Add the **spice** mixture (it will splutter) and briskly stir-fry for a minute or so, then stir-fry in the curry paste, tomato purée, ketchup, plum tomatoes, minced and chopped chilli and curry base gravy. When simmering, transfer to a 4¹/₂ pint (2.6 l) lidded casserole and put it into the oven.

Now 'seal' the meat by stir-frying it in the pan, with the rest of the ghee or oil, for about 10 minutes. Drain off any liquid (keep it for stock or use later), then put the hot meat into the casserole dish. Stir well, put on the lid and replace the dish in the hot oven. After about 20 minutes inspect, stir and add a little heated stock or water if needed.

Continue to cook for another 20 minutes, then test for tenderness. Add the garam masala and the fresh cor-iander and cook for at least 10 more minutes. When the meat is as tender as you want it, and just prior to serving, spoon off any excess oil. Salt to taste and serve.

MADRAS CURRY

— ◆ —

Like *phal*, this is another restaurateur's invention.

Serves: 4

1½ lb (675 g) stewing steak
  or lamb, diced
4 tablespoons ghee or
  vegetable oil
2 teaspoons hot curry paste
  (page 5)
1 tablespoon tomato ketchup
2 fresh tomatoes, chopped
6 red chillies, finely chopped
½ green pepper cut into ½
  inch (1.25 cm) diamonds
½ teaspoon dry fenugreek
  leaves

2 pints (1.2 l) curry base
  gravy (page 16)
1 tablespoon ground
  almonds
2 teaspoons lemon juice
2 teaspoons garam masala
1 tablespoon chopped fresh
  coriander leaves

SPICES

2 teaspoons coriander
1½ teaspoons cummin
1 teaspoon chilli powder

Preheat the oven to 375°F/190°C/Gas 5. Mix the **spices** with 2 tablespoons of water. Heat half the ghee or oil in a pan. Add the spice mixture (it will splutter) and briskly stir-fry for a minute or so, then stir-fry in the curry paste, ketchup, tomatoes, chillies, green pepper, fenugreek and curry base gravy. When simmering, transfer to a 4½ pint (2.6 litre) lidded casserole and put it into the oven.

Now 'seal' the meat by stir-frying it in the pan with the rest of the ghee or oil, for about 10 minutes. Drain off any liquid (keep it for stock or use later) then put the hot meat into the casserole dish. Stir well, put on the lid and replace in the hot oven.

After about 20 minutes inspect, stir and add a little heated stock or water if needed. Continue to cook for another 20 minutes, then test for tenderness. Add the ground almonds, lemon juice, garam masala and fresh coriander and cook for at least 10 more minutes. When the meat is as tender as you want it, and just prior to serving, spoon off excess oil. Salt to taste and serve.

HOT DHANSAK

— ◆ —

Unlike the authentic Parsee/Bombay dish, many restaurants jack up the 'heat' level. I've taken that liberty.

Serves: 4

12 oz (350 g) stewing steak or lamb, diced

4 tablespoons ghee or vegetable oil

1 tablespoon hot curry paste (page 5)

2 tablespoons tomato ketchup

2 fresh tomatoes, chopped

6 green chillies, chopped

1½ teaspoons dry fenugreek leaves

2 pints (1.2 l) curry base gravy (page 16)

2 teaspoons brown sugar

4 tablespoons cooked red lentils (masoor)

8 oz (225 g) canned ratatouille

2 teaspoons garam masala

1 tablespoon chopped fresh coriander leaves

SPICES

1½ teaspoons coriander

1 teaspoon cummin

1 teaspoon chilli powder

1 teaspoon paprika

½ teaspoon turmeric

⅓ teaspoon mango powder

Preheat the oven to 375°F/190°C/Gas 5. Mix the **spices** with 2 tablespoons of water. Heat half the ghee or oil in a pan. Add the spice mixture (it will splutter) and briskly stir-fry for a minute, then stir-fry in the curry paste, ketchup, tomatoes, chillies, fenugreek and curry base gravy. When simmering, transfer to a 4½ pint (2.6 litre) lidded casserole and put it into the oven.

Now 'seal' the meat by stir-frying it in the pan, with the rest of the ghee or oil, for about 10 minutes. Drain off any liquid (keep it for stock or use later), then put the hot meat into the casserole. Stir, cover and replace in the hot oven.

After about 20 minutes inspect, stir and add a little stock or water if needed. Continue to cook for another 20 minutes, then add the remaining ingredients. Cook for at least 10 minutes. When the meat is tender and just prior to serving, spoon off excess oil. Salt to taste and serve.

HOT AND SWEET PATIA

Like *dhansak*, *patia* is another mild Parsee dish which restaurants like to serve chilli-hot. Its red sweet sauce can pack a punch as hot as you like.

Serves: 4

1¹/₂ lb (675 g) stewing steak
4 tablespoons ghee or vegetable oil
1 tablespoon hot curry paste (page 5)
1 tablespoon tomato purée
1 tablespoon tomato ketchup
2 or 3 canned plum tomatoes
2-3 tablespoons minced red chilli (page 60)
1 tablespoon brown sugar
1 tablespoon vinegar (any kind)
2 pints (1.2 l) hot curry base gravy (page 16)
salt to taste

SPICES

¹/₂ teaspoon mustard seeds
¹/₂ teaspoon fennel seeds
¹/₂ teaspoon cummin seeds
¹/₄ teaspoon fenugreek seeds

Preheat the oven to 375°F/190°C/Gas 5. Mix the **spices** with 2-3 tablespoons of water. Heat half the ghee or oil in a pan. Add the spice mixture (it will splutter) and briskly stir-fry for 20 seconds, then stir-fry in the other ingredients (except the salt). When simmering, transfer to a 4¹/₂ pint (2.6 litre) lidded casserole and put it into the oven.

Now 'seal' the meat by stir-frying it in the pan, with the rest of the ghee or oil, for about 10 minutes. Drain off any liquid (keep it for stock or use later), then put the hot meat into the casserole dish. Stir well, put on the lid and put the dish in the hot oven. After about 20 minutes inspect, stir and add a little heated stock or water if needed.

Continue to cook for another 20 minutes then inspect again, this time testing for tenderness – it will probably need a little longer. When the meat is as tender as you want it, and just prior to serving, spoon off any excess oil. Salt to taste, garnish and serve.

CHAPTER · 4

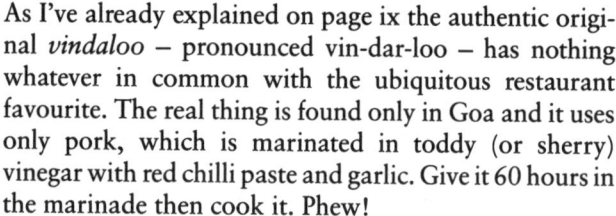

Meat Specialities

Our voyage around the world's hot curry lands takes us in this chapter to Jamaica, Africa, Pakistan, India, Burma, Thailand and Indonesia to bring together eight hot curries, each as different as can be. Pork, beef, lamb, goat, offal and mince are the principals, and the spices are totally authentic, designed to harmonise precisely with each dish. You're unlikely to find any of them at the standard curry house, but try them and you'll be hooked.

GOAN PORK VINDALOO

As I've already explained on page ix the authentic original *vindaloo* – pronounced vin-dar-loo – has nothing whatever in common with the ubiquitous restaurant favourite. The real thing is found only in Goa and it uses only pork, which is marinated in toddy (or sherry) vinegar with red chilli paste and garlic. Give it 60 hours in the marinade then cook it. Phew!

Serves: 4

1¹/₂ lb (675 g) diced lean
    pork (fresh, not frozen)
3 tablespoons ghee or
    vegetable oil
4 garlic cloves, finely
    chopped
1 inch (2.5 cm) piece fresh
    ginger, finely chopped
6 oz onion, finely chopped
6 fl oz (175 ml) water
4 fl oz (100 ml) dry red wine
2 fl oz (50 ml) dry to
    medium sherry
2 tablespoons lemon juice
1 tablespoon garam masala
    (page 4)
1 tablespoon chopped fresh
    coriander

MARINADE
4 fl oz (100 ml) toddy or
    sherry vinegar
2 tablespoons minced red
    chilli (page 60)
1 teaspoon turmeric
2 teaspoons salt
1 teaspoon crushed black
    peppercorns

SPICES
15-20 dried tiny birdseye red
    chillies
10 cloves
6 green cardamoms
2 inch (5 cm) piece cassia
    bark
1 teaspoon cummin seeds

Mix the marinade ingredients together thoroughly in a large non-metallic bowl and add the pork. Cover and refrigerate for 24 hours.

To cook the pork, preheat the oven to 375°F/190°C/ Gas 5. Heat the ghee or oil in a pan (karahi, wok or frying pan). Stir-fry the garlic for 20 seconds, then add the ginger and 20 seconds later add the onion. Now add the **spices** and stir-fry on a lowish heat for 15 minutes. Add spoonfuls of water to prevent sticking as needed. Transfer this mixture to a 4¹/₂ pint (2.6 l) minimum lidded casserole dish. Drain the pork and discard the marinade, then add the pork, 6 fl oz water, the red wine, sherry and lemon juice to the casserole. Stir well, put on the lid and place the dish in the oven.

After 20 minutes inspect, stir and add a little stock or water if needed. Cook for another 20 minutes then check again. After an hour the pork should be nearly tender. Add the garam masala and fresh coriander and cook for at least 10 more minutes. When tender, and just before serving, spoon off excess oil. Salt to taste and serve.

SORPOTEL

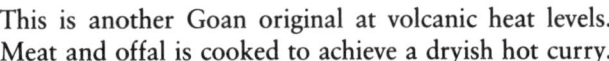

This is another Goan original at volcanic heat levels. Meat and offal is cooked to achieve a dryish hot curry.

Serves: 4

1 lb (450 g) lean diced pork
4 oz (110 g) lamb heart, diced
4 oz (110 g) lamb liver, diced
2 tablespoons vegetable oil
6 garlic cloves, very finely chopped
1 inch (2.5 cm) cube fresh ginger, very finely chopped
8 oz (225 g) onion, very finely chopped
2 tablespoons minced green chilli (page 60)
12 fl oz (350 ml) water
4 tablespoons wine vinegar

7 fl oz (200 ml) canned coconut milk
1 tablespoon chopped fresh coriander leaves
salt to taste

SPICES

1¹/₂ teaspoons cummin seeds
8 cloves
2 star anise
4 green cardamoms
2 inch (5 cm) piece cassia bark
1 teaspoon turmeric

Cut the pork into thin strips about 1¹/₂ inches × 1 inch × ¹/₄ inch (3.75 cm × 2.5 cm × 6 mm).

Heat the oil in a karachi or wok. Stir-fry the garlic for 20 seconds, then add the ginger and 20 seconds later the **spices**. Stir-fry for a further 20-30 seconds, then add the pork, the onion and chilli. Lower the heat and sizzle this mixture for 10 minutes, adding the occasional spoonful of water as needed.

Add the heart and liver and stir-fry for a further 10 minutes, then add the 12 fl oz (350 ml) water and the vinegar. Stir well. Continue to cook for another 20 minutes, then inspect, testing for tenderness. Add the coconut milk and the fresh coriander and cook for at least 10 more minutes. When it is as tender as you want it, and just prior to serving, spoon off any excess oil. Salt to taste, garnish and serve.

THAI LAMB GREEN CURRY

Fragrancy in Thai curries comes from lemon grass, lime leaves and shrimp paste. The green colour comes from fresh basil, coriander and green chillies.

Serves: 4

1¹/₂ lb (675 g) lean lamb, cut into 1¹/₂ inch (4 cm) cubes
4 tablespoons vegetable oil
4 garlic cloves, chopped
1 tablespoon shrimp paste (kapi)
1 inch (2.5 cm) cube fresh galingale or ginger, chopped
8 oz (225 g) onion, chopped
1 green capsicum, deseeded and chopped
6-12 green cayenne chillies, destalked

4 tablespoons spring onion leaves, chopped
2 tablespoons chopped fresh coriander leaves
2 fresh or dried lemon grass stalks
6-8 whole fresh basil leaves
6 fresh or dried lime leaves (if available)
2 tablespoons fish sauce (nam-pla)
14 fl oz (400 ml) canned coconut milk

Preheat the oven to 375°F/190°C/Gas 5. Heat the oil in a karahi or wok. Stir-fry the garlic, shrimp paste, galingale or ginger and onion for 10 minutes. Let it cool then mulch it down in the food processor or blender with the green capsicum, chillies, spring onion leaves and coriander, using sufficient water to obtain a pourable paste. Pour it back into the karahi and stir-fry on medium heat for about 5 minutes, adding more water to prevent sticking.

In a 4¹/₂ pint (2.6 l) lidded casserole combine the stir-fry and the meat. Stir well. Put on the lid and put the dish into the hot oven. After about 20 minutes inspect, stir and add a little hot water if needed. Continue to cook for another 20 minutes, then add the remaining ingredients. It should be fairly runny so add hot water if necessary. Cook for another 10 minutes or so, or until the meat is as tender as you want it. Salt to taste and serve.

PIRI PIRI BEEF

— ◆ —

The African word for chilli is *piri-piri* (or *pili-pili/peri-peri* etc). In Kenya, Uganda and Tanzania are found the tiny red piercingly hot Ugandan (bird) chillies with which the Asian community evolved their own style of curry.

Serves: 4

1½ lb (675 g) lean stewing steak, diced
3 tablespoons vegetable oil
4 garlic cloves, chopped
2 inch (5 cm) cube fresh ginger, chopped
2 tablespoons minced green chilli (page 60)
4 oz (110 g) onion, chopped
10 or more fresh or dried red bird Ugandan chillies
14 oz (400 g) canned consommé or clear soup

1 yellow pepper, cut into strips
8 cherry tomatoes
1 teaspoon extra hot chilli powder
1 tablespoon garam masala
1 tablespoon chopped fresh coriander leaves
salt to taste

SPICES
1 teaspoon cummin seeds
1 teaspoon mustard seeds
1 teaspoon turmeric

Heat the oil and stir-fry the garlic and ginger for about 30 seconds. Add the **spices**, then the minced chilli and stir-fry these for another minute. Add the onion, the chillies and the consommé. Simmer for 10 minutes or so.

Preheat the oven to 375°F/190°C/Gas 5. Meanwhile, 'seal' the meat in a 4½ pint (2.6 l) lidded casserole dish. Add the stir-fry, pepper and tomatoes. Stir well, put on the lid and put into the hot oven. After 20 minutes stir and add a little heated stock or water if needed.

Continue to cook for another 20 minutes, then inspect again, this time testing for tenderness – it will probably need a little longer. Add the chilli powder, garam masala and the fresh coriander and cook for at least 10 more minutes. When the meat is tender, and just prior to serving, spoon off excess oil. Salt to taste and serve.

REDANG DAGING

— ◆ —

Indonesia has a population which includes Chinese and Indians. The national dish reflects this. It is a hot beef curry of curry spices, and of course chilli, with ground peanut paste and soy sauce. Unique and delicious!

Serves: 4

1¹/₂ lb (675 g) lean meat
(beef, lamb etc), cubed
3 oz (75 g) unsalted raw
peanuts
5 fl oz (150 ml) milk
2 oz (50 g) creamed coconut
2 tablespoons vegetable oil
6 garlic cloves, finely sliced
1 inch (1.25 cm) cube fresh
ginger, finely sliced
8 oz (225 g) onion, sliced
6–8 whole green chillies

1 tablespoon minced red
chilli (page 60)
2 teaspoons soy sauce
1 tablespoon whole fresh
coriander leaves

SPICES
1¹/₂ teaspoons coriander
1 teaspoon cummin
1 teaspoon turmeric
1 teaspoon chilli powder
1 teaspoon curry powder

Put the peanuts and **spices** into the blender and mulch down into a paste using enough water to make it easy to pour. Heat the milk and melt the coconut block in it.

Heat the oil in a kahari or wok and stir-fry the garlic for 20 seconds. Add the ginger, then after 20 seconds add the spicy paste, then the onion. Simmer for 10 minutes.

Preheat the oven to 375°F/190°C/Gas 5. Meanwhile, seal the meat in a 4¹/₂ pint (2.6 l) casserole dish. Add the whole chillies and the minced chilli and ¹/₂ pint (300 ml) water. Stir well. Put on the lid and put the dish into the hot oven. After about 20 minutes inspect, add the spicy peanut paste and coconut milk and add a little heated stock or water if needed. Mix well and return to the oven.

Cook for another 20 minutes, then add the soy sauce and fresh coriander and cook for at least 10 more minutes. When the meat is as tender as you want it, and just before serving, spoon off excess oil. Salt to taste and serve.

WEST INDIAN GOAT

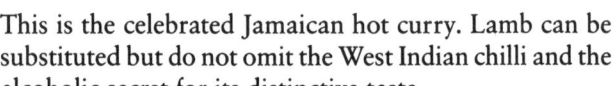

This is the celebrated Jamaican hot curry. Lamb can be substituted but do not omit the West Indian chilli and the alcoholic secret for its distinctive taste.

Serves: 4

1¹/₂ lb (675 g) lean leg of lamb or goat, cubed
3 tablespoons vegetable oil
4 garlic cloves, chopped
8 oz (225 g) onion, finely chopped
2 tablespoons hot curry paste (page 5)
¹/₂ red pepper, cut into diamonds
4 Haberno (Bahamian) chillies, quartered
2 slices canned pineapple, cubed

1 teaspoon brown sugar
2-3 teaspoons bottled West Indian chilli sauce
2 fl oz (50 ml) white rum
salt to taste

SPICES
1 teaspoon coriander seeds
2 brown cardamoms
2 inch (5 cm) piece cassia bark
1 teaspoon fennel seeds
¹/₂ teaspoon lovage seeds

Preheat the oven to 375°F/190°C/Gas 5. Heat the oil in a karahi or wok and add the **spices,** garlic, onion and curry paste. Stir-fry for 10 minutes. Transfer to a 4¹/₂ pint (2.6 l) lidded casserole, adding the meat and all the other ingredients (except the salt) with a cupful of water. Stir well, put on the lid and put the dish into the hot oven.

After about 20 minutes inspect, stir and add a little heated stock or water if needed. Continue to cook for another 20 minutes, then inspect again, this time testing for tenderness – it will probably need a little longer and cook for at lest 10 more minutes. When the meat is as tender as you want it, spoon off any excess oil. Salt to taste, garnish and serve.

PAKISTANI MIRCHI KEEMA

— ◆ —

Mince is economical and indestructible in the cooking. This superb hot and savory recipe from the Frontier deliciously proves it.

Serves: 4

1¹/₂ lb (675 g) lean mince
3 tablespoons ghee or vegetable oil
4 garlic cloves, finely chopped
8 oz (225 g) onion, finely chopped
1 tablespoon hot curry paste (page 5)
4 canned plum tomatoes
1 tablespoon tomato ketchup
7 fl oz (200 ml) canned tomato soup
4-6 green chillies, shredded

1-2 tablespoons garam masala (page 4)
1 tablespoon dried fenugreek leaves
1 tablespoon chopped fresh coriander leaves
salt to taste

SPICES
2 teaspoons cummin seeds
1 teaspoon mustard seeds
1 teaspoon ground coriander
1 teaspoon turmeric
1-3 teaspoons chilli powder
¹/₂ teaspoon cardamom seeds

Preheat the oven to 375°F/190°C/Gas 5. Heat the oil in a karahi or wok and add the **spices**, garlic, onion and curry paste. Stir-fry for 5 minutes. Add the mince and stir-fry for 5-10 minutes. Transfer it all to a 4¹/₂ pint (2.6 l) lidded casserole, adding the tomatoes, ketchup, soup and chillies. Stir well, put on the lid and put the dish into the hot oven. After about 20 minutes inspect, stir and add a little heated stock or water if needed. Continue to cook for another 20 minutes, then add the garam masala to taste and the fenugreek and fresh coriander and cook for at least 10 more minutes. Just prior to serving, spoon off any excess oil. Salt to taste, garnish and serve.

BURMESE MEAT CHILLI FRY

—— ◆ ——

Burmese curries are piquant and often tempered with coconut. This one is no exception. The result is a dry dish which is delicious with lentils and Indian bread.

Serves: 4

1¹/₂ lb (675 g) lean stewing
    steak, cut into 1¹/₂ inch (4
    cm) cubes
4 tablespoons vegetable oil
4 garlic cloves, very finely
    chopped
1 inch (2.5 cm) cube fresh
    ginger, very finely chopped
6 oz (150 g) onion, finely
    chopped
1 tablespoon hot curry paste
    (page 5)
1 cup plain white flour
1 beef stock (Oxo) cube
¹/₂ cup hot water
10 or more whole red
    birdseye chillies, fresh or
    dried
1 tablespoon tomato purée
7 fl oz (200 ml) canned
    coconut milk

1 tablespoon garam masala
    (page 4)
1 tablespoon dried fenugreek
1 tablespoon chopped fresh
    coriander

GARNISH
some chippings of fresh
    coconut (or a sprinkling of
    desiccated)

SPICES
1¹/₂ teaspoons coriander
    seeds
1 teaspoon cummin seeds
¹/₄ teaspoon fennel seeds
pinch of fenugreek seeds
6 cloves
4 green cardamoms
1 teaspoon extra hot chilli
    powder (optional – more if
    you like!)

Preheat the oven to 375°F/190°C/Gas 5. Heat half the oil in a karahi or wok and add the **spices**, garlic, ginger, onion and hot curry paste. Stir-fry for 5 minutes.

Heat a 4¹/₂ pint (2.6 l) lidded casserole on the stove top and add the remaining oil. Dunk the meat cubes in the flour, put them into the casserole and stir-fry for 5-6

minutes. Dissolve the stock cube in half a cup of hot water. Add it to the meat with the chillies and the tomato purée. Add the fried paste of spices, onion and garlic. Stir well, put on the lid and put the dish into the hot oven.

After about 20 minutes inspect, stir and add a little heated stock or water if needed. Continue to cook for another 20 minutes, then add the garam masala, fenugreek and fresh coriander and cook for at least 10 more minutes. Just prior to serving, spoon off any excess oil. Salt to taste, garnish with the fresh coconut and serve.

Opposite page 32 (top to bottom): Chilli Chapatti (**page 59**), and Guinea Fowl Hot Pot Roast (**page 41**)

Opposte (top to bottom): Patrani Mirch Machli (**pages 42-3**), Minced Red Chilli (**pages 60-1**), and Tulsi Aur Anardana Maachli (**page 46**)

———◈———

CHAPTER 5

Poultry Specialities

Our worldwide journey around the curry lands continues in this chapter with a collection of eight poultry dishes, each carefully selected to give you the widest possible contrast in tastes and textures.

GOAN CHICKEN RECHEADE

——— ◆ ———

Another superb Goan recipe. Recheade is a red chilli and toddy vinegar based paste.

Serves: 4

$1^{1}/_{2}$ lb (675 g) chicken breast, skinned, filleted and cut into $1^{1}/_{2}$ inch (4 cm) cubes
4 garlic cloves, chopped
10-12 red cayenne chillies, chopped
4 fl oz (100 ml) sherry (or wine) vinegar
3 tablespoons vegetable oil

6 fl oz (150 ml) red wine
1 tablespoon brown sugar
1 tablespoon garam masala
1 tablespoon chopped fresh coriander

SPICES
1 teaspoon cummin seeds
1 teaspoon coriander
1 teaspoon chilli powder

Put the garlic, chillies and vinegar into the blender and mulch to a paste. Use a little water if needed.

Heat the oil in a large karahi or wok. Add the **spices**

and stir-fry for 30 seconds and add the chicken. Stir-fry for 5 minutes or so, then add the spice paste. Simmer for 10 more minutes, stirring occasionally and adding a little water if needed to prevent sticking. Add the red wine, sugar, garam masala, fresh coriander and salt to taste. Stir-fry for 5 more minutes, then garnish and serve.

MOORGI MOULI OR MOLLEE

The mouli originated in Mexico ten thousand years ago.

Serves: 4

1¹/₂ lb (675 g) chicken breast, skinned, filleted and cut into 1¹/₂ inch (4 cm) cubes

3 tablespoons sesame oil

2 garlic cloves, finely chopped

4 oz (110 g) onion, finely chopped

1 tablespoon hot curry paste (page 5)

6-10 fresh green cayenne chillies, sliced

14 fl oz (400 ml) canned coconut milk

1 tablespoon whole fresh coriander leaves

20 strands saffron

salt to taste

SPICES

2 teaspoons mustard seeds

1 teaspoon turmeric

1 teaspoon sesame seeds

1-2 teaspoons black peppercorns

Heat the oil in a large karahi or wok and stir-fry the garlic and onion for around 10 minutes to brown them. Add the **spices** and paste and stir-fry for a further 3 minutes. Now add the chicken pieces and stir-fry briskly until they turn white all over. Reduce the heat and add the chillies and coconut milk, then simmer for 10 minutes, stirring from time to time. It must be fairly runny, so add a little water as needed. Add the fresh coriander, saffron and salt to taste. Simmer for about 10 more minutes, garnish then serve.

SINGAPORE SLING

— ◆ —

It's hot chicken curry, spiced Singaporean style with an alcoholic kick!

Serves: 4

1¹/₂ lb (675 g) chicken breast, skinned, filleted and cut into 1¹/₂ inch (4 cm) cubes
3 tablespoons vegetable oil
2 garlic cloves, finely chopped
6-12 fresh mixed red and green chillies
1 tablespoon green peppercorns in brine
1 tablespoon vinegar (any type)
6 oz (175 g) onion, finely chopped

2 tablespoons hot curry paste (page 5)
1 tablespoon mango chutney, finely chopped
6 fl oz (175 ml) stock or water
4 fl oz (100 ml) brandy
1 teaspoon soy sauce
water from a coconut
3 tablespoons minced coconut flesh
6-8 fresh basil leaves, chopped
salt to taste

Heat the oil in a large karahi or wok. Add the garlic, then 30 seconds later add the chillies and green peppercorns, stir-frying continuously. One minute later add the vinegar and onion, then reduce the heat and let it simmer for 10-15 minutes so that it becomes golden brown.

Add the curry paste, mango chutney and stock or water. When simmering, add the chicken and cook for 15 minutes. Add the secret weapon – the alcohol – and the soy sauce, coconut water and flesh, and basil leaves. It should not be too dry, so control it with a little water as needed. Simmer for 10 more minutes. Salt to taste, garnish and serve.

MIRCHWANGAN MURGH

— ◆ —

A fiery hot deep red chicken curry from Kashmir.

Serves: 4

1½ lb (675 g) chicken breast, skinned, filleted and cut into 1½ inch (4 cm) cubes
3 tablespoons vegetable oil
4 garlic cloves, finely chopped
8 oz (225 g) onion, finely chopped
½ red pepper, sliced
20 fresh crimson or dried Kashmiri chillies
1 tablespoon garam masala (page 4)

1 tablespoon chopped fresh coriander leaves
salt to taste

MARINADE
1 tablespoon bottled tandoori paste
1 tablespoon extra hot chilli powder
2 fl oz (50 ml) bottled beetroot vinegar
1 bottled beetroot, sliced
1 tablespoon minced red chilli (page 60)
4 fl oz (100 ml) red wine

Mulch the marinade ingredients down to a pouring paste in the blender, using water as needed. Mix the marinade and chicken cubes in a non-metallic bowl, cover and refrigerate for up to 48 hours.

To cook, heat the oil in a large karahi or wok and stir-fry the garlic for 30 seconds. Add the onions and stir-fry for 5 minutes, then add the chicken and all the marinade. Stir as needed for 5 minutes, adding a little water if needed to prevent sticking. Add the remaining ingredients and continue cooking for around 15 more minutes. Salt to taste, garnish and serve.

Note: Ensure the chicken is fresh and has never been frozen when marinating it for 48 hours in the fridge.

MURGH SIXER

— ◆ —

'So hot it will knock you for six' says its creator, India's Top Chef, Satish Arora.

Serves: 4

1¹/₂ lb (675 g) chicken breast, skinned, filleted and cut into 1¹/₂ inch (4 cm) cubes
oil for deep-frying
3 tablespoons ghee
3 garlic cloves, sliced
1 inch (2.5 cm) cube fresh ginger, sliced
6-10 fresh red cayenne chillies
4 oz (110 g) yoghurt
salt to taste

MARINADE
3 tablespoons minced red chilli (page 60)
2 garlic cloves, finely chopped

2 oz (50 g) plain white flour
1 oz (25 g) cornflour
3 eggs
2 tablespoons chopped fresh coriander leaves
¹/₂ teaspoons ground cummin

SPICES
1 teaspoon cummin seeds
8-10 curry leaves, fresh or dried
1 teaspoon turmeric

GARNISH
6-10 green chillies, sliced longways and fried
fresh coriander leaves

Mulch down the marinade ingredients in the blender to obtain a pouring paste, using water as needed. Mix the marinade and chicken cubes in a non-metallic bowl. Cover and refrigerate for between 1 and 4 hours.

To cook, heat the deep-frying oil to 375°F/190°C, then place the marinated chicken pieces in one by one. Deep-fry for 10 minutes, until crisp. Meanwhile, heat the ghee in a large karahi or wok. Add the **spices,** and 20 seconds later add the garlic, ginger and chillies. Stir-fry for 3 minutes, then add the hot deep-fried chicken pieces and the yoghurt. Simmer for 5 minutes. Salt to taste, garnish with the sliced chillies and coriander leaves, and serve.

NEPALESE RIVER DUCK

— ◆ —

A rare spicy recipe from the Gurkha tribes of Nepal.

Serves: 4

1¹/₂ lb (675 g) duck breast, skinned, filleted and cut into 1¹/₂ inch (4 cm) cubes
4 tablespoons vegetable oil
4 garlic cloves, finely chopped
1 inch (2.5 cm) cube fresh ginger, thinly sliced
6 oz (175 g) onion, thinly sliced
1 tablespoon hot curry paste (page 5)
2-4 tablespoons chilli pickle, chopped (page 61)
6 tomatoes, chopped

4 oz (110 g) mushrooms, chopped
1 tablespoon chopped fresh or 1 teaspoon dried mint
1 tablespoon garam masala (page 4)
¹/₂ pint (300 ml) single cream
3 tablespoons breadcrumbs
salt to taste

SPICES
1 teaspoon mustard seeds
1 teaspoon sesame seeds
¹/₂ teaspoon wild onion seeds
¹/₂ teaspoon fennel seeds
¹/₂ teaspoon fenugreek seeds

Heat the oil in a large karahi or wok. Fry the **spices** for 30 seconds. Add the garlic and stir-fry for 30 seconds more, then add the ginger and 30 seconds after that add the onion. Stir-fry for about 10 minutes so that it becomes golden, adding a spoonful of water now and again to prevent sticking. Add the curry paste.

Preheat the oven to 375°F/190°C/Gas 5. Transfer the spice mixture to a 4¹/₂ pint (2.6 l) lidded casserole. Add the duck, pickle, tomatoes and mushrooms, put on the lid and put the dish into the hot oven. After 20 minutes, add the mint, garam masala, cream and breadcrumbs. Stir and return to the oven. Inspect after 15 more minutes. It should be perfectly tender and richly creamy. Salt to taste and serve.

THAI TURKEY ORANGE CURRY

— ◆ —

This fragrant Thai curry works well with turkey.

Serves: 4

1½ lb (675 g) turkey breast or leg, skinned, filleted and cut into 1½ inch (4 cm) cubes
3 tablespoons vegetable oil
4 garlic cloves, finely chopped
1 tablespoon shrimp paste (kapi)
1 inch (2.5 cm) cube fresh galingale or ginger, chopped
1 medium sized carrot, shredded
1 yellow pepper, chopped
12 orange red chillies, chopped

6 fl oz (175 ml) canned cream of tomato soup
2 fresh or dried lemon grass stalks
2 tablespoons fish sauce (nam-pla)
7 fl oz (200 ml) canned coconut milk
6 whole fresh basil leaves
6 or more fresh green chillies, sliced
6 fresh or dried lime leaves
1 tablespoon whole fresh coriander leaves
salt to taste

Heat the oil in a large karahi or wok. Stir-fry the garlic and galingale or ginger for about 10 minutes. Let it cool then mulch it down in the food processor or blender with the carrot, pepper and chillies, using sufficient water to obtain a pourable paste. Pour it back into the karahi and stir-fry on medium heat for about 5 minutes, adding water spoon by spoon to prevent any sticking.

Add the turkey pieces and stir frequently, ensuring they are being cooked on all sides. After 10 minutes, add the tomato soup, lemon grass, fish sauce and coconut milk. Keep stirring and ensure it is always fairly runny – add a little water if needed. After a further 5 minutes add the basil, green chillies, lime leaves and coriander, and a little water if needed. After a further 5 minutes or so the turkey should be ready. Salt to taste and serve.

HOT POT ROAST

— ◆ —

Whole duck, chicken or game bird, coated in a thick hot spicy paste, studded with peppercorns and roasted.

Serves: 4

1 × 4 lb (1.8 g) duck or roasting bird, skinned
1 lb (450 g) fresh spinach, finely shredded
3 tablespoons mixed peppercorns (pink, white and black)
20 cloves
10 fresh red cayenne chillies, sliced longways
7 fl oz (200 ml) canned consomée
2 teaspoons minced garlic
1 tablespoon minced red chilli (page 60)
1 tablespoon garam masala

SPICES
2 star anise
2 inch (5 cm) cassia bark
2 teaspoons cummin seeds
4 brown cardamoms
1 teaspoon coriander seeds
$^1/_2$ teaspoon fennel seeds

MARINADE
16 oz (450 g) Greek yoghurt
2 tablespoons garam masala
1 tablespoon chilli powder
2 tablespoons chopped fresh coriander
1 teaspoon dried mint
4 garlic cloves, chopped
cornflour if needed

Mulch down the marinade ingredients in the blender to get a thick paste. If too thin add some cornflour.

Wash the bird inside and out, and dry with kitchen paper. Cram the cavity with the spinach and **spices**.

Preheat the oven to 375°F/190°C/Gas 5. Place the bird on an oven tray and generously coat it with marinade. Stud all over with peppercorns (as many as you like), cloves and chillies. Cook for 20 minutes, then cover loosely with kitchen foil. Cook for a further 45 minutes. Now discard the foil and pour any juices into a karahi or wok. Return the bird to the oven for a final 20-30 minutes. Remove from the oven to rest for 10 minutes before carving. Add any further juices and the consommé to the karahi and bring to the boil, then add the garlic, minced chilli and garam masala. Stir-fry for 8-10 minutes to reduce to a pourable gravy. Salt to taste. Serve with the meat and stuffing.

CHAPTER · 6

Seafood Dishes

Fish and shellfish and spices go hand in hand. These six recipes show how true that is, and how much variety of taste, texture and appearance there can be. The only thing they have in common is heat.

PATRANI MIRCHI MACHLI

—— ◆ ——

White fish coated in a green herb and chilli purée and steamed or baked.

Serves: 4

4 pieces filleted and skinned
   pomfret or cod steak, each
   about 8 oz (225 g)
6 oz (175 g) onion, chopped

COATING
2 bunches fresh coriander
   leaves, plus tender stalks
2 tablespoons minced green
   chilli (page 60)
4 garlic cloves, chopped

1 teaspoon ground cummin
$^1/_2$ teaspoon salt
$^1/_4$ teaspoon lovage seeds
$^1/_4$ teaspoon asafoetida
2 tablespoons vinegar (any
   type)

GARNISH
desiccated coconut
lemon wedges

Put the onion in a small pan with about half a cup of water and gently simmer for 10 minutes or so. Cool enough to put in the blender with the coating ingredients and mulch to achieve a pourable paste like thick porridge. Add water if necessary, or if it is too wet put it in a sieve to drain.

If baking the fish, preheat the oven to 375°F/190°C/Gas 5. If steaming, set a steamer tray above a large pan of simmering water.

Lay each piece of fish on a large piece of foil, then cover completely with paste, using up all the paste. Wrap the fish pieces tightly in the foil and place them on an oven tray. Bake or steam for 15 minutes.

To serve, carefully unwrap and discard the foil. The coating should have adhered to the fish and should be quite moist. Pour all or some of the liquid from the tray over the dish. Garnish with a light sprinkling of desiccated coconut and lemon wedges.

Note: Instead of foil you could wrap the fish in banana or patra leaves. Bake or steam in the same way.

THAI RED CURRY FISH

— ◆ —

A red hot paste coated fish, spiced in the Thai style and grilled to perfection.

Serves: 4

4 salmon fillets, each about
    8 oz (225 g), skinned
6 oz (175 g) onion, chopped

COATING
6 canned plum tomatoes
1 tablespoon tomato purée
2 tablespoons minced red
    chilli (page 60)
2 teaspoons paprika
2 tablespoons fish sauce
    (nam-pla)

1 tablespoon shrimp paste
    (kapi)
1/2 red capsicum pepper,
    chopped
4 garlic cloves, chopped
4 tablespoons coconut milk
    powder

GARNISH
fresh red chillies, thinly sliced
garam masala (page 4)
basil leaves, shredded

Put the onion in a small pan with about half a cup of water and gently simmer for 10 minutes or so. Cool enough to put in the blender with the other coating ingredients and mulch to achieve a pourable paste like thick porridge. Add water if necessary, or if it is too wet put it in a sieve to drain.

Preheat the grill to medium hot. Line the grill tray with kitchen foil (to catch drips and make cleaning up easier), then put the grill rack into the tray. Put the pieces of fish on to the rack, close together, and coat the top side of the fish with half of the marinade. Place the tray at the midway position and grill for 5-8 minutes (depending on actual heat level). The fish should then be cooking but not burning. Turn the pieces of fish, keeping them close together, and coat the other side with the remaining marinade. Repeat the grilling. Sprinkle with the garnish ingredients and serve.

SRI LANKAN BALLICHOW

— ◆ —

Fish chunks or prawns simmered in a tart hot brown sauce.

Serves: 4

$1^1/_2$ lb (675 g) fish fillets or steak (any type), cut into 2 inch (5 cm) cubes, or shelled raw prawns (any type)
3 tablespoons vegetable oil
4 garlic cloves, finely chopped
2 tablespoons hot curry paste (page 5)
5 fl oz (150 ml) tomato juice
1 tablespoon minced red chilli (page 60)
1 tablespoon tomato purée
4 fl oz (100 ml) medium sherry

4 tablespoons vinegar (any type)
1 tablespoon chopped fresh coriander leaves
salt to taste

SPICES
1 teaspoon black mustard seeds
1 teaspoon sesame seeds
$^1/_2$ teaspoon ajowain seeds

GARNISH
green chilli, finely chopped
fresh coconut shreds

Heat the oil in a large karahi or wok. Fry the **spices** for 20 to 30 seconds, then add the garlic and 30 seconds later add the curry paste. Stir-fry for 2-3 minutes, then add the tomato juice, chilli and tomato purée. When simmering add the fish or prawns and stir-fry for 8-10 minutes, keeping it loose but not runny by adding a little water as needed. Add the remaining ingredients and simmer for a further 5 minutes or until the fish or prawns are cooked. Salt to taste, garnish with the chopped chilli and coconut shreds and serve.

TULSI AUR ANARDANA MAACHLI

— ◆ —

Pomfret fillets in red chilli paste, meuniered then enhanced with basil and pomegranate, in another dish from Master Chef Satish Arora. If pomfret is not available use sole, turbot, halibut or shellfish.

Serves: 4

4 pomfret skinned fillets, each about 8 oz (225 g)
2 tablespoons plain white flour for dusting
3 tablespoons vegetable oil
2 tablespoons olive oil
salt to taste

MARINADE
2 tablespoons minced red chilli (page 60)
2 garlic cloves
1 teaspoon turmeric
2 tablespoons fresh lime juice

GARNISH
2 garlic cloves, finely chopped
1 inch (2.5 cm) cube fresh ginger, shredded
6 cherry tomatoes, quartered
4 green chillies, chopped
6 basil leaves, chopped
1 tablespoon pomegranate seeds, crushed
1 teaspoon cummin seeds, lightly crushed
12 whole coriander leaves

Mulch down the marinade ingredients in the blender, using enough water to obtain a pourable paste. Pour over the fillets and set aside to marinate for 30 minutes.

Heat the vegetable oil in a large flat frying pan. Dust the fillets with a little flour and fry for 5-8 minutes, then turn carefully and continue for a further 5 minutes so that both sides are cooked.

Meanwhile, heat the olive oil in a separate pan, then add the garnish ingredients and just singe them for no more than a minute. Arrange the fish on an oval serving platter, squeeze on the lime juice and sprinkle with some salt and the singed garnish. Serve at once.

BANGLADESH ACHAR CHINGRI

— ◆ —

King Prawns simmered in a golden garlic and chilli pickle sauce.

Serves: 4

24 *raw king prawns, total weight 1¹/₂ lb (675 g) after thawing, peeling and de-veining*
3 *tablespoons blended mustard oil*
2 *garlic cloves, chopped*
1 *inch (2.5 cm) cube fresh ginger*
4 *oz (110 g) onion, chopped*
1 *tablespoon chopped fresh coriander leaves*
2 *tablespoons bottled garlic pickle*
1 *tablespoon chilli pickle (page 61)*

2 *tablespoons vinegar (any type)*
2 *tablespoons ghee*
salt to taste

SPICES
1 *teaspoon coriander seeds*
1 *teaspoon mustard seeds*
¹/₂ *teaspoon wild onion seeds*
¹/₂ *teaspoon turmeric*

GARNISH
fresh coriander leaves
fresh red chillies, sliced
lemon wedges

Heat the oil in a karahi or wok. Add the garlic, ginger, onion and coriander and stir-fry on low heat until brown (about 15 minutes). Allow to cool enough to put into the food processor. Add the garlic pickle, chilli pickle and vinegar and mulch with enough water to obtain a thick smooth paste.

Clean the karahi and heat the ghee. Stir-fry the **spices** and add the paste, then lower the heat and briskly stir-fry for 5 minutes, adding a little water to prevent sticking. Add the prawns and stir occasionally, adding a little more water if necessary, until they are cooked (about 10-12 minutes). Salt to taste and serve with the garnish.

FISH XACUTTI

Another superb Goan dish, in a brilliant bright yellow sauce. The correct pronunciation is Zacuetee.

Serves: 4

4 white fish fillets (any type), each about 8 oz (225 g)
3 tablespoons vegetable oil
6 garlic cloves, minced
1 inch (2.5 cm) cube fresh ginger, finely chopped
2 oz (50 g) onion, very finely chopped
1 coconut, water and flesh
6-8 fresh green chillies, chopped
6-8 curry leaves, fresh or dried
8 cherry tomatoes

1 tablespoon fresh coriander leaves
salt to taste

SPICES
2 teaspoons white poppy seeds
1/2 teaspoon fennel seeds
2 star anise
1 blade mace
6 small dried chillies, chopped
4 cloves
4 green cardamoms

Heat the oil in a large flat frying pan and stir-fry the **spices** for 30 seconds. Add the garlic, ginger and onion and continue stir-frying for about 1 minute more. Now add the coconut water topped up with water to make 7 fl oz (200 ml) in total. When simmering add the chillies, curry leaves, tomatoes and fish fillets. Simmer for 10 minutes, ensuring that the fish is covered with the liquid. Add a little water spoon by spoon to prevent sticking.

While the fish is simmering, grate the fresh coconut flesh into shreds. When the simmering time is up, add 2-3 tablespoons of the coconut to the pan, with the coriander. Salt to taste and serve after a further 3-4 minutes.

Opposite (top to bottom): Stuffed Chillies (**page 50**), Red Chilli Raita (**page 63**), and Sabz-Ze-Zaar (**page 54**)

Opposite page 49 (top to bottom): Baked Potato Surprise (**page 55**), and Coconut Raita (**page 63**). Alongside are Haberno, Jalapēno and cayenne chillies (**pages xi-xii**)

CHAPTER 7

Hot Vegetable Dishes

Vegetables should not be omitted from your menu. Not only are they good nutritionally, but they taste excellent – especially when boosted with 'heat'. Indeed, this relatively small number of recipes may surprise you by their versatility and variety.

MUSHROOM CHETINAD

— ◆ —

Simple but effective mushroom-chilli combination from South India.

Serves: 4

1¹/₂ lb (675 g) button mushrooms, cleaned and sliced

4 tablespoons vegetable oil

1 tablespoon black mustard seeds

4 tablespoons dried onion flakes

2 tablespoons hot curry paste (page 5)

6 fl oz (175 ml) tomato juice

1 tablespoon tomato ketchup

2 tablespoons minced red chilli (page 60)

1 tablespoon garam masala (page 4)

salt to taste

Heat the oil in a large karahi or wok. Add the mustard seeds and dry onion flakes and stir-fry briskly for 20 seconds, then add the curry paste and stir-fry for a further 20 seconds. Pour in the tomato juice to stop the frying, then add the mushrooms and remaining ingredients. Cook for just 5 minutes, stirring from time to time. Serve.

STUFFED CHILLIES

Large mild chillies stuffed with spicy mashed potato, parsnip and peas.

Serves: 4

8 large green (Anaheim) chillies, each at least 6 inch (15 cm) long by 1¹/₂ inch (4 cm) wide at the top end
slivers of red chilli to garnish

FILLING
1 tablespoon ghee plus a little extra for brushing
1 teaspoon cummin seeds
2 garlic cloves, minced
1 teaspoon hot curry paste (page 5)
12 oz (350 g) mashed potato
1 tablespoon chopped fresh coriander leaves
1 tablespoon chopped fresh mint leaves

4 fresh green chillies, chopped

SAUCE
2 tablespoons vegetable oil
2 garlic cloves, minced
4 oz (110 g) onion, very finely chopped
1 tablespoon hot curry paste (page 5)
1 tablespoon minced red chilli (page 60)
7 fl oz (200 ml) canned consommé
1 tablespoon garam masala
salt to taste

Cut a slit down most of the length of each chilli. Keep the stalk on but carefully remove the pith and the seeds. To make the filling heat 1 tablespoon ghee in a karahi or wok. Stir-fry the cummin for 20 seconds, then add the garlic and 30 seconds later the paste. When sizzling, add the other filling ingredients. Mix well and allow to cool. Stuff the chillies with the mixture.

Put the chillies on an oven tray, brush with ghee and bake for 12-15 minutes at 375°F/190°C/Gas 5.

Make the sauce during this time. Heat oil in a small pan, add the garlic and onion and stir-fry for about 5 minutes. Add the paste and chilli, and when sizzling the consommé and garam masala. Salt to taste. Put the peppers in a serving bowl and pour the sauce over them. Garnish with the red chilli slivers and serve.

CHILLI MASALA VEGETABLE STIR FRY

— ◆ —

Ghetto blasting heat level if you want it, and all done in 15 minutes!

Serves: 4

1¹/₂ lb (675 g) prepared vegetables of your choice – for example, 4 oz (110 g) each of the following: potatoes, boiled and cubed; carrots, boiled and cubed; frozen peas, thawed; canned sweetcorn, drained; mange tout, topped and tailed; asparagus tops

3 tablespoons vegetable oil
4 garlic cloves, minced
8 oz (225 g) onion, finely chopped
1 tablespoon hot curry paste (page 5)

1 cup canned sweetcorn liquid or stock and/or water
6 or more fresh red cayenne chillies, chopped
1 tablespoon garam masala (page 4)
salt to taste

SPICES
1 teaspoon cummin seeds
1 teaspoon coriander seeds
1 teaspoon mustard seeds
¹/₂ teaspoon lovage seeds
¹/₃ teaspoon fenugreek seeds
¹/₃ teaspoon fennel seeds

Heat the oil in a large karahi or wok. Stir-fry the **spices** for 20 second, then add the garlic. Thirty seconds after that add the onion and stir-fry for 5 minutes. Add the curry paste and sizzle it in for another minute. Add the cup of liquid, and when that is simmering add the chillies and the vegetables. They simply need the occasional stir and in 5 minutes they're ready. Add the garam masala, salt to taste, and finish off with a quick burst on full heat. Serve at once.

VEGETABLE CALDINE

— ◆ —

Goan hot and coconut creamy combination.

Serves: 4

1¹/₂ *lb (675 g) prepared
vegetables of your choice –
for example, 6 oz (175 g)
each of the following:
small broccoli florettes,
blanched; Kenyan beans,
topped and tailed;
courgettes, sliced; canned
chickpeas, drained*
3 tablespoons vegetable oil
4 garlic cloves, chopped
*1 inch (2.5 cm) cube fresh
ginger, chopped*
8 oz (225 g) onion, chopped
12 cherry tomatoes, halved
*2 tablespoons minced green
chilli (page 60)*

*2 tablespoons red lentils,
soaked and drained*
*7 fl oz (200 ml) canned
coconut milk*
*2 tablespoons vinegar (any
type)*
12 fresh coriander leaves
salt to taste

SPICES
1 teaspoon cummin seeds
1 teaspoon coriander seeds
¹/₂ teaspoon turmeric

GARNISH
*Red chillies, shredded
fresh coconut flakes or
desiccated coconut*

Heat the oil in a large karahi or wok and stir-fry the
spices, garlic, ginger and onion for 15 minutes on low
heat until golden brown. Cool enough to mulch down in
the blender, adding water to make a thick pourable paste.

Heat a cup of water in the karahi. Add the tomatoes,
minced chilli, lentils and spicy paste, then add the vegetables and stir fry for a few minutes until they are very
nearly cooked. Add the coconut milk, vinegar and coriander leaves and give it a final simmer. Salt to taste,
garnish with the shredded chillies and coconut and serve
at once.

KUAL-LA-DA

— ◆ —

Malaysian peppery vegetable curry.

Serves: 4

12 oz (350 g) aubergine
3 tablespoons vegetable oil
8 oz (225 g) onion, very
  finely chopped
1 tablespoon tamarind or
  lemon juice
15 fl oz (500 ml) vegetable
  stock or water
4 oz (110 g) bean sprouts
6 oz (175 g) Chinese leaves,
  shredded
3 sticks celery

1 tablespoon chopped fresh
  coriander leaves
1 teaspoon soy sauce
salt to taste

PASTE
4 garlic cloves, chopped
24 raw cashew nuts
2 tablespoons minced red
  chilli (page 60)
1 teaspoon turmeric

Chop the aubergine into 1 inch (2.5 cm) cubes and immerse them in salty water for half an hour. Mulch the paste ingredients down in the blender using water as needed.

Heat the oil in a large karahi or wok. Stir-fry the onion until golden brown (about 10 minutes), then add the paste and stir-fry for 2-3 minutes adding a little water as needed to prevent sticking. Add the tamarind or lemon juice and stock or water, and when simmering, add the aubergine (discard the salty water), bean sprouts, Chinese leaves and celery. After 5 minutes add the coriander leaves and soy sauce. Salt to taste and serve at once.

SABZ-ZE-ZAAR

—— ◆ ——

A hot mixed vegetable dish from Hyderabad.

Serves: 4

12 oz (350 g) small
  cauliflower florettes
¹/₂ teaspoon turmeric
3 tablespoons ghee or
  vegetable oil
4 garlic cloves, minced
1 inch (2.5 cm) cube fresh
  ginger, shredded
8 oz (225 g) onion, very
  finely chopped
1 tablespoon minced red
  chilli (page 60)
1 lb (450 g) fresh spinach,
  shredded
1 red pepper, thinly sliced
6 whole green chillies
¹/₂ pint (300 ml) vegetable
  stock or water
8 oz (225 g) yoghurt
salt to taste

SPICES
2 teaspoons coriander seeds
1 teaspoon fennel seeds
12 green cardamoms, seeds
  only
2 inch (5 cm) piece cassia
  bark
2 star anise
4 cloves
4 bay leaves
12 curry leaves, dried or
  fresh

GARNISH
2 oz (50 g) fresh coconut,
  shredded
6 quail eggs, hard boiled and
  halved
raw cashew nuts, fried
fresh mint leaves

Blanch the cauliflower in ample boiling water with the turmeric. Drain. Heat a small pan without oil. Put in the **spices** and 'roast' them for 1 minute. Cool and grind.

Heat the ghee or oil in a large karahi or wok. Stir-fry the garlic for 30 seconds, then add the ginger and 30 seconds later the onion. Stir-fry for 10 minutes.

Add 2-3 tablespoons water and the ground **spices**, then add the minced chilli and when sizzling add the stock or water and the yoghurt. Bring to the simmer. Add the spinach, red pepper and whole chillies and when soft add the cauliflower. Simmer until the vegetables are cooked to your liking. Salt to taste, garnish and serve at once.

BAKED POTATO SURPRISE

A hot paste coating surrounds a large potato. The surprise comes from the fact that a chilli is inserted inside!

Serves: 4

4 large baking potatoes
4 long green chillies

PASTE
4 garlic cloves, chopped
24 raw cashew nuts
2 tablespoons dried onion flakes

1 tablespoon hot curry paste (page 5)
1 tablespoon minced red chilli (page 40)
1 tablespoon garam masala (page 4)
$1/2$ teaspoon salt

Mulch down the paste ingredients in the food processor, using minimal water to make a thick paste. Pre-heat the oven to 375°F/190°C/Gas 5.

Wash and dry the potatoes and drill a hole in them longways, using an apple corer. Insert a whole chilli in each. Coat the potatoes with the paste, then wrap them quite tightly in kitchen foil. Bake for 1 hour. Check whether they are cooked by piercing with a small knife or skewer (don't unwrap the foil). Continue baking if needed. Serve when ready.

HOT BOMBAY POTATO

The restaurant favourite, pepped up into hot gear. Put $1/2$ teaspoon turmeric in the boiling water before adding the potatoes – they'll be a gorgeous yellow colour.

Serves: 4

$1^1/_2$ lb (675 g) potatoes,
   peeled, boiled and cut into
   bite-sized cubes
4 tablespoons vegetable oil
1 teaspoon cummin seeds
4 garlic cloves, minced
4 oz (110 g) onion, very
   finely chopped

1 tablespoon hot curry paste
   (page 5)
1 teaspoon brown sugar
6 cherry tomatoes, sliced
2 red chillies, chopped
2 green chillies, chopped
salt to taste

Heat the oil in a large karahi or wok. Fry the cummin seeds for 30 seconds, then add the garlic and 30 seconds later add the onion, stir-frying continuously. After 5 minutes add the hot curry paste and brown sugar. Keep stirring for a further 5 minutes, adding water spoon by spoon to prevent sticking. Add the tomatoes and chillies, and when soft add the potato. Stir until the potatoes are hot, continuing to add water as required. Salt to taste and serve.

SAMBAR MALABAR

—— ◆ ——

A runny lentil and vegetable curry with a kick in its tail.

Serves: 4

4 tablespoons red masoor
   lentils, split and polished
2 tablespoons gram flour
   (besan)
1 tablespoon coconut milk
   powder
3 tablespoons vegetable oil
4 garlic cloves, finely
   chopped
8 oz (225 g) onion, finely
   chopped
1 teaspoon hot curry paste
   (page 5)
1½ pints (900 ml) water
1 large carrot, cut into small
   cubes
3 oz (75 g) parsnip, cut into
   small cubes
2 oz (50 g) potato, cut into
   small cubes

10 whole fresh red chillies
2 tablespoons tamarind or
   lemon juice
1 tablespoon vinegar (any
   type)
1 tablespoon chopped fresh
   coriander leaves
6-8 curry leaves, fresh or
   dried
½ teaspoon salt
a few whole coriander leaves
   to garnish

SPICES

1½ teaspoons mustard seeds
1 teaspoon black peppercorns
½ teaspoon coriander seeds
¼ teaspoon fenugreek seeds
¼ teaspoon asafoetida

Soak the lentils for 10 minutes and drain. Mix the gram flour and coconut powder with enough water to make a runny paste.

Heat the oil in a large saucepan and fry the **spices** for 20 second. Add the garlic and stir-fry for 30 seconds, then add the onion and continue stir-frying for 5 minutes. Add the curry paste and when it sizzles carefully add the water and bring to the simmer. Add the drained lentils and all the remaining ingredients except the coriander leaves. Simmer for 20 minutes, garnish with the coriander leaves and serve.

CHAPTER 8

Accompaniments

Accompaniments . . . without which no curry, hot or mild, is complete! Most of these accompaniments, however, *are* hot and are designed to fine-tune your volcanic level to incendiary. The only exceptions are the raitas, designed to be the antidote to excess piquancy.

MUSTARD RICE

Spiky mustard seeds and black pepper with contrasting cooling coconut fried in chilli oil spice make this a gorgeous rice.

Serves: 4

10 oz (300 g) Basmati rice	**SPICES**
1 pint (600 ml) water	1 teaspoon mustard seeds
3 tablespoons ghee	1 teaspoon black
4 oz (110 g) button	peppercorns
mushrooms, chopped	$^1/_2$ teaspoon fennel seeds
1 tablespoons desiccated	4 fresh green chillies,
coconut	chopped

Soak the rice in cold water for 20 minutes. Rinse it several times to remove the dust and starch. Drain. Bring the measured water to the boil.

Heat the ghee in a saucepan. Stir-fry the **spices** for 20 seconds, then add the drained rice and stir-fry for a minute or so. Add the boiling water, stir and put on the lid. Lower the heat to medium. As soon as the water has absorbed into the rice (4-6 minutes) remove the pan from the heat.

Add the mushrooms and coconut to the rice, mix in well and put the pan in a warm place (not on direct heat) with the lid on. Leave it for between 30 and 60 minutes for the grains to become separated (the longer you leave it, the better). Just before serving, fork through the rice to aerate and separate the grains.

CHILLI CHAPATTI

— ◆ —

The celebrated flat bread, given a 'fuel-injected' stuffing.

Makes: 4 chapattis

1 lb (450 g) brown ata (chapatti) or wholemeal flour
1/2-1 cup water

1 teaspoon cummin seeds, roasted
1 tablespoon minced green chilli (page 60)

Mix the flour and water together in a large bowl, working it until it becomes an elastic, cohesive lump. Leave it for about 15 minutes.

Knead the dough, then divide it into four and make each piece into a sphere. Roll out one sphere into a 4 inch (10 cm) disc. Shape it into a purse and put a quarter of the filling inside. Press it shut and roll it into a 6 inch (15 cm) disc. Repeat with the other three spheres of dough.

Heat a flat pan to very hot. Using no oil, cook each chapatti on both sides until it has no 'raw' patches and has black/brown 'blisters'. Serve hot.

FRESH CHILLI TASSELS

— ◆ —

Just to garnish the dish – fuel the fire, so to speak.

These are easily made, using fresh chillies of any size or colour. Leave the stalks on. Cut a bit below the stalk, longways towards and right through the tip. Make several cuts. Immerse in a bowl of cold water containing ice cubes for 30-60 minutes and the tassels will form. Drain and use at once.

Finished tassels can be seen in the photograph opposite page 17.

VINEGARED CHILLIES

— ◆ —

Simply fresh green or red chillies in vinegar. Nothing more, nothing less. Lasts for ever.

Use only very fresh chillies. Put them, stalks and all, into a lidded jar, then fill the jar to the brim with distilled clear vinegar. Leave for a few days before using, or keep for as long as you wish.

MINCED GREEN OR RED CHILLIES

— ◆ —

No cooking. Instant. Immortal.

¹/₂ lb (225 g) red or green   *distilled clear vinegar*
chillies (but not mixed
colours)

Destalk the chillies. Put them in the food processor and pulse, adding just enough vinegar to obtain a coarse purée.

To store, put into a clean lidded jar and top off with more vinegar. The purée can be used at once or days – even years – later.

GREEN CHILLI PICKLE

— ◆ —

Cooking required. This large batch lasts a while and is worth the effort. Adapted from a recipe by Curry Club member Trevor Pack.

1 lb (450 g) fresh green
  chillies
1/2 pint (300 ml) vegetable oil
6 garlic cloves, finely
  chopped
1 inch (2.5 cm) cube fresh
  ginger, finely chopped
1 1/2 lb (675 g) onions, finely
  chopped
1 tablespoon muscavado
  sugar

1 tablespoon salt
1/2 pint (300 ml) distilled
  clear vinegar

SPICES
4 tablespoons ground
  cummin
2 tablespoons turmeric
1 tablespoon hot curry paste
  (page 5)

Make a paste of the **spices** by adding water. Heat the oil in a large saucepan. Add the garlic, ginger and onions and stir-fry for 5 minutes, then add the paste and stir-fry for a further 10 minutes. Add the chillies, sugar, salt and vinegar and simmer for a further 15 minutes.

Let it cool a little then bottle in hot clean lidded jars. Top up with a little hot oil before lidding. Can be eaten at once, but improves greatly with age.

SWEET RED CHILLI CHUTNEY

— ◆ —

Another cooked recipe. The combination of sweet and hot puts mango chutney into touch!

1 lb (450 g) fresh red chillies
6 fl oz (175 g) water
8 oz (225 g) sugar
2 garlic cloves, chopped
2 or 3 bay leaves

5 fl oz (150 ml) distilled
  white vinegar
1¹/₂ teaspoons wild onion
  seeds

Place the water and sugar in a 2¹/₄ pint (1.4 l) saucepan and dissolve the sugar completely on a low heat. Raise the heat, add all the remaining ingredients and bring to the boil. Immediately lower the heat to achieve a gently rolling simmer. At first it will seem very watery, but it quickly reduces and begins to caramelise. It is cooked after about 20 minutes, when it will have set to a syrupy texture. During the 20 minutes, inspect and stir three or four times. Remove the pan from the heat and let it cool sufficiently to bottle in sterilised jars. It will keep almost indefinitely.

RAITA

— ◆ —

Yoghurt-based instant chutneys are usually served with any curry meal. Raitas are normally very mild and the most effective antidote to very hot tastes on the mouth. Water, as we saw on page xvi, is less effective. Here are three raitas – one for heat fanatics, and the final two the mild antidotes to the previous 59 searing recipes.

CHILLI RAITA

— ◆ —

5 oz (150 g) Greek yoghurt
3 or 4 fresh green or red
  chillies, chopped

Simply mix, chill and serve.

COCONUT RAITA

— ◆ —

5 oz (150 g) Greek yoghurt   *2 tablespoons coconut milk*
3 tablespoons fresh coconut,   *powder*
  shredded   *coconut flakes to garnish*

Simply mix, chill and serve.

PLAIN RAITA

— ◆ —

Simply unflavoured natural Greek yoghurt, served
chilled.

INDEX